Clips And Quips

For
Midnight Oil Sermons
and Last Minute
Sunday School Lessons

366 Language Tools
For Preachers And Teachers

Douglas B. Bailey

CSS Publishing Company, Inc., Lima, Ohio

CLIPS AND QUIPS FOR MIDNIGHT OIL SERMONS
AND LAST MINUTE SUNDAY SCHOOL LESSONS

Copyright © 2001 by
CSS Publishing Company, Inc.
Lima, Ohio

Some scripture quotations are from the *New Revised Standard Version of the Bible*, copyright 1989 by the Division of Christian Education of the National Council of the Churches of Christ in the USA. Used by permission.

Some scripture quotations are from the *Revised Standard Version of the Bible*, copyrighted 1946, 1952 ©, 1971, 1973, by the Division of Christian Education of the National Council of the Churches of Christ in the USA. Used by permission.

Library of Congress Cataloging-in-Publication Data

Bailey, Douglas B., 1935-
    Clips and quips for midnight oil sermons and last minute Sunday school lessons : 366 language tools for preachers and teachers / Douglas B. Bailey.
        p.   cm.
    Includes bibliographical references.
    ISBN 0-7880-1797-7 (alk. paper)
    1. Homiletical illustrations. I. Title.
BV4225.3 .B35 2001
251'.08—dc21   00-065114
                                                                        CIP

For more information about CSS Publishing Company resources, visit our website at www.csspub.com.

ISBN 0-7880-1797-7   PRINTED IN U.S.A.

To Gerry —

trip planner, traveling companion, and Lake Erie fishing partner,
teacher and maker of music at the piano and organ,
wife, mother, and grandmother par excellence,

whose rich imagination in writing lively children's musicals
added greatly to her husband's desire and determination
to pursue and complete this writing project

Table Of Contents

Introduction:
How This Book Can Help You

I am aware that glancing at this book's title on the cover could lead to possibly a first *but false* impression regarding what sort of "writer's work ethic" this author would recommend to you. So I would quickly make it clear to any morally scrupulous reader that this book is not intended in any way to be an enthusiastic approval or sweeping endorsement of waiting until the eleventh hour to prepare midnight oil sermons and last minute Sunday school lessons. But perhaps the book title caught your attention because (let's be perfectly honest!) at one time or another we as pastors and teachers do end up helplessly entangled in frantic, last minute preparation of sermons and church school class materials. And there are those times when we get completely bogged down and totally frustrated in getting ready to preach or teach, because we simply can't come up with a suitable illustration or colorful example desperately needed to perk up our presentation. This book is a collection of approximately 360 metaphors, analogies, descriptive phrases, and a variety of language "gimmicks" which I offer to you as visual and descriptive language to help make your sermons and lesson plans more vividly appealing, clear, and relevant to sanctuary worshipers and classroom participants. Most of these "clips and quips" are language tools that I either created myself or else borrowed and adapted from various sources for use in my sermons over a 38-year period. Some items, however, have been newly contrived for inclusion in this book.

I deliberately chose *not* to describe this book's contents as "sermon or teaching illustrations," because typical illustrations for preaching and teaching usually consist of stories, life episodes, or object lessons written in a narrative form. Instead of narrative materials that tell a story in the manner of a "teaching parable," I have attempted to create metaphorical models, imagery-laden analogies, and other modes of descriptive language that can make religious concepts and themes more understandable and down-to-earth. A key goal in worship and education is to help church members make a truly satisfying connection between "Sunday morning *message*" and "Monday morning *meaning*." And so we definitely need to improve our capability to come up with metaphors, analogies, and other language tools that can enable people in our congregations to have an intelligent and sensitive "feel" for what gives the gospel message its authenticity, relevance, and vitality.

The language tools in this book are "writer's aids and devices" intended to serve a variety of purposes. Some of these language tools make use of metaphors and analogies, such as the atomic energy metaphorical model, to portray what are the vital dynamics or "innards" that give real life credibility to spiritual concepts and themes. For example, the underlying reality and dynamics of salvation through Christ's sacrifice on the cross are compared to the pattern of how power is released through the splitting of the atom. Also there are visual images used to provide colorful examples of various spiritual concerns, such as the descriptive picture of "the wild stampede of reindeer in the department stores' annual Christmas Derby" for use in reference to the flagrant, razzle-dazzle commercialism typical during the Christmas season. Furthermore, I have devised language tools to make the insights of some well established conceptual and theoretical frameworks applicable for use in sermons and Christian education, such as Karl Barth's understanding of the Trinity, James Fowler's faith development theories, the Transactional Analysis Parent-Adult-Child model of personality, or the Theory X and Theory Y management styles of how managers deal with employees in the world of business. In addition, some key themes from theological and spiritual authors such as Elizabeth Johnson, Sallie McFague, Howard Thurman, Elton Trueblood, and Leslie Weatherhead have inspired the creation or borrowing of visual language. Finally, there are other language tools in this collection that may not fit into a neat and precise category but simply are "word gimmicks" that I have found useful for one reason or another.

Although a particular tool may work perfectly well all by itself in reference to a particular theme or topic, some "writer's devices" may be much more effective when used in sets or combinations including more than one language tool. For example, the atomic energy metaphors or the Transactional Analysis visual images may be more effective when used in combinations, such as (1) "splitting of the atom," "chain reaction," and "cobalt therapy," or (2) Good Shepherd, Shrewd Saint, and Natural Child of God. Some of the language tools are presented to be used intentionally in paired combinations — for example, "eye" and "ear," "God's very best" and "life's very worst," "maximum results" and "minimum expectations," etc. Also it is possible to use the same language tool in a variety of different contexts, and there are some specific "word gimmicks" that appear several times in this text, including, for instance, "the very best vs. the very worst," "the more you learn, the less you know," and "weaving the threads and fabrics of old patterns into new patterns."

As part of the church's educational ministry, language tools can help church members grasp a more meaningful appreciation of (1) the dynamics of how God's saving power functions in human life, (2) the significance of various events and situations described in the Bible, and (3) the implications of how to live a meaningful life as a Christian in today's world. With this in mind, the materials in this book have been divided into four major sections with language tools selected to facilitate our understanding of:

1. how we can believe there really is a God who has power to make an impact in human life;
2. how we can believe that Jesus truly accomplished a victory for us through his life, crucifixion, and resurrection;
3. how the process of God's saving power deals effectively with the futility and agony of human existence;
4. the dynamics and dimensions of what living the Christian life is all about.

This fourth section on "living the Christian life" includes language tools in reference to:

1. establishing through prayer a vital relationship with God;

2. growing in faith throughout the span of a lifetime;
3. facing the realities of life and death;
4. becoming mature in the life of discipleship;
5. understanding how the church is called to carry out its mission;
6. developing effective personal relationships in the life of the home and elsewhere as part of daily living.

The contents of these four sections have been arranged in *an outline format* to enable the reader to find more easily whatever categories and topics are of special interest, i.e., Christmas, the cross of Jesus, the meaning of suffering, implications of the resurrection, etc. I need to explain that instead of starting first with a comprehensive outline of spiritual themes and topics and then selecting or creating an array of language tools to correspond to each segment of such an outline, my approach as an author was to locate and compile "language tool" material already contained in my sermons, and then arrange this, along with some additional new items, in a conceptual framework suited to the material selected. So, because of my approach, there are some interesting and important themes and topics not mentioned or included. It would be a most worthwhile challenge in another writing venture to start out with a specific theme or an overall conceptual framework (i.e., "baptism," "doctrine of the Holy Spirit," etc.) and then design language tools to use in connection with that theme or framework.

This collection of "clips and quips" is like a department store with a highly diverse variety of merchandise, not all of which can be expected to meet the needs of every customer. You will want to shop around and look for those particular items in this book that you find both pleasing and worthwhile. I hope these tools will trigger your imagination to develop your own set of visual images, "word gimmicks," etc., and — *equally important* — to adapt and revise this book's resources for other creative purposes not envisioned here. In addition to whatever resources you find here that you would like to try on for size, your imagination is bound to come up with many other possible alternatives for using language tools to bring new life to the pulpit and the classroom.

The Clips And Quips Collection

I. Language tools in reference to our understanding of the nature of God

A. The mystery of God as the Divine Spirit

1. **airpower:** We can describe God's "Spirit" as God's *airpower* that can make things happen like a mighty wind which is invisible yet powerful. Our rationale for this can be based upon the New Testament Greek word *pneuma* which can mean "wind" or "spirit." True spirituality involves contact with the powerful stuff of God's invisible airpower. Unfortunately, for many people "spirituality" is a word that indicates the stale and boring atmosphere of spiritual *stuffiness* instead of anything *truly dynamic and powerful* like a mighty breath of invigorating, fresh air.

2. **box of our limited understanding:** Many of Jesus' parables warn us that the mysterious ways of God often do not make sense according to our typical expectations of "how things are supposed to be." God is not bound and gagged and tied up inside a pint-size, airtight box of human logic with its cramped quarters and narrow dimensions designed according to the strict limits and severe specifications of our human understanding.

3. **fear of God:** There is more than one way in which persons can experience the fear of God. For some persons such as Ebenezer Scrooge, a man totally insensitive and oblivious to the consequences of his self-centered lifestyle, the fear of God may be experienced as a providential "wake-up call" in the form of a sudden panic attack evoking the overwhelming dread of a death sentence to be carried out in the most terrifying manner by "hell's firing squad."
   The Psalms (for example, Psalms 6, 22, and 88) show that the fear of God also can be experienced as a horrifying sense of lonely

abandonment like a gallows' trap door opening under our feet as a complete surprise, with no advance warning whatsoever, and we are left hanging with no reassuring, firm foundation of meaning on which to stand. Such was the abandonment felt by Jesus hanging on the cross as he cried out, in the words of Psalm 22:1, "My God, my God, why have you forsaken me?"(Matthew 28:46; Mark 16:33).

Furthermore, the fear of God can be experienced as "holy stage fright," such as Moses felt in the presence of the burning bush. Just as a child feels nervous and afraid whenever a loved one opens a clumsily wrapped gift the child hopes will be truly pleasing and acceptable, so we as God's children can experience the holy stage fright of hoping anxiously that God will be receptive and look favorably upon us when in prayer we open up, with fumbling fingers and with stumbling words, our clumsily wrapped gift to God of our real selves with all our rough edges, shortcomings, and weaknesses.

4. **fire:** The song "Spirit of the Living God,"[1] often sung at church camp, contains the words "melt me, mold me ..." — a reminder that God is indeed like the *fire* in a furnace which *melts* raw material into something that can be *molded* into a useful tool or a beautiful work of art. When we consider the biblical reference to the God who is like a refiner's fire (i.e., Malachi 3:2-3), we can realize why prayer can be at times a painful experience, as we go through a "melt-down" that brings out *the best* in us by purging and purifying *the worst* in us.

5. **"I REALLY am who I am!":** God's awe-inspiring, magnificent statement to Moses that "I AM WHO I AM" (Exodus 3:14) could be restated and reinterpreted as including and revealing an *additional* humorous, joyful dimension of the loving and mysterious God who with a smiling face says playfully to Moses and to us, "I REALLY am who I am!"

6. **mercy is mighty, not mushy:** The mercy of God is not watered-down, mushy sentimentality. Instead of a cheap dose of pain relief

aimed at blunting our sensitivity to harsh reality, God's mercy makes us strong enough to face the harsh, painful truth of our shortcomings. We can face even the worst faults that are deep within us, because God's mercy assures us that *it is not the end of the world* to take a long hard look at ourselves. God's mercy gives us confidence to believe that through our painful confession of what we are *at our worst* we are set free to grow toward what we can be *at our best.*

7. **"mysterious ways" or "peculiar habits":** When people's ways of doing things don't make sense, we pay them the compliment of having "mysterious ways" *if* we find these ways delightfully charming. However, *if* we find people's strange ways of doing things to be frustrating or obnoxious to us, we may write these people off as having "peculiar habits." Similarly, whenever God's ways of doing things may not make sense to us, we need to be honest with our feelings in our prayers and "tell it like it is" — indicating whether God's strange ways of doing things seem like intriguing "mysterious ways" that inspire us or frustrating "peculiar habits" that irritate us.

8. **mystery of life is rooted in the mystery of God:** Each of God's gifts to us is a reminder of God's mysterious presence in our lives because God is a "self-giving God" and there is something of God's personal self *mysteriously intermingled* with each God-given gift. Life is a gift from God, and so to be aware of the mystery of *life* is also to be aware of the mystery of *God.*

9. **supercharged awareness of God:** The result of clearing obstacles clogging the lifeline between us and God is that this makes possible an increased flow of spiritual energy accompanied by a *supercharged awareness* of God's presence. And we need to remain in the presence of God long enough to be blessed with a supercharged, intense awareness of God. This is true, *regardless of whether or not* the blessing of an intense awareness of God includes also an intense awareness of God's *specific dream for our lives.*

13

On one hand, there will be times when we have *no vision whatsoever* of what lies ahead, but a supercharged, intense awareness of God's companionship can give us the patience and the strength to keep walking forward and to keep waiting for a surprise from God to appear ahead on the horizon. But, on the other hand, whenever we are truly blessed with a most vivid vision of something ahead in the future that could bring out the best in us, *this should never be taken lightly*, as it may be certainly a living proof that we are indeed living at present in the abundantly supercharged presence of God. When we do actually find ourselves to be supercharged and fired up with an intense, authentic dream of *the best that is yet to be*, we should ask God to help keep the lifeline open, so that we can maintain a supercharged, energizing companionship with God and thereby increase our strength and determination to pursue God's dream for us.

10. **the more we learn (about God), the less we know:** The closer we get to God, the more we are aware how much we do not understand the mystery of God's ways. When "the more we learn the less we know" about God, the more we need God's peace which is *beyond all understanding* — God's reassuring peace which more than compensates for our lack of knowledge and understanding regarding the mystery of God's ways.

11. **tiger turned into tabby cat:** The consequence of watering down the awesome dimensions of God's holiness is to change a tiger into a tabby cat.

12. **wind of God's spirit:** The mighty yet often gentle wind of God's spirit can transform even the tiniest spark of our feeble, fickle faith into the steady flame of a more vibrant faith. The ashes and coals and sad remains of a lost faith can be changed by the breath of God into a magnificent fire that can shed both the light of truth and the warmth of love. The prevailing wind of God's Spirit can breathe into our lives new purpose, new creativity, and new commitment which can transform the spark of human potential into the flame of human fulfillment. Prayer is how we keep the doors and windows of our lives open to the wind of God's Spirit.

B. Counting upon God to be dependable and trustworthy

1. flight pattern of our lives and wind currents of God's spirit: The flight pattern of our lives is upheld safely and surely by the wind currents of God's spirit whenever we surrender ourselves to God's guidance and direction. In this way the flight pattern of our lives becomes merged with God's jet stream pattern of *something greater than ourselves.*

2. floating bridge: God makes it possible for us to walk safely on a floating bridge over our life's troubled waters.[2] This bridge is not completely finished before we start walking on it. It is constructed by God plank by plank as we walk forward step by step, trusting God to support and sustain us as needed in the midst of trouble, until finally both we and our floating bridge reach solid ground as God successfully engineers the triumphant conclusion of our present day crisis.

3. fog of our confusion: The dense fog of our perplexity and confusion is removed only by the blazing warmth of God's love plus the penetrating light of God's truth giving our lives meaning and direction. It takes both the warmth of love and the light of truth to eliminate this fog and cause it to evaporate completely. The light of truth without love and the warmth of love without truth are powerless to dispel clouds of ignorance and insensitivity. And so the thickest layers of this fog can be penetrated and banished only by God's power which is an inseparable, invincible mixture of love and wisdom.

4. God's *best*: God's *best that is yet to be* is the joyful end result of faith's lifelong journey. God's *best that is right now* helps us day by day and moment by moment to continue this journey in a spirit of joyful adventure and thanksgiving. God's *best that was yesterday* is now a precious memory giving us joyful reassurance that the God who leads us through our fragile early years and our vulnerable middle years will never let the frailties and infirmities of our later years deny us either God's *best that is right now* or God's

15

best that is yet to be. We have joy because from one day to the next God's *best* is ever surprisingly new, wonderously different, and yet to be counted upon as steadfast, eternal and everlasting — yesterday, today, and tomorrow.

5. **God's faithfulness when we fumble:** God is there to grab us whenever we fumble and stumble, after we have gotten ourselves way out on a shaky, wobbly, fragile limb as part of the risks of being faithful servants.

6. **God's holy love:** God's justice and mercy are never incompatible opposites, so that God would ever be forced to choose between being a merciless, law-enforcing courtroom judge or a wishy-washy, unjust compromiser. Instead, the God of *holy love* is able always to extend justice as an act of mercy and to extend mercy in a way that creates a just and righteous outcome. God is able simultaneously to do what is *just and right*, plus make things *mercifully* right, "bright and beautiful."[3]

7. **God's roles as the Father-Mother Parent, as Lover, and as Friend:** As the *Father-Mother Parent*, God can be counted upon repeatedly to get us off to a new start in life at a new level of maturity and to watch over and nurture us while we are still maturing and adjusting to the new role God has given us. As *Lover*, God can be counted upon repeatedly to save us and empower us through love that passionately reaches out to us, feels and shares our ups and downs with deepest intensity, goes all out to set us free from our sin's downward spiral headed toward death and oblivion, and never gives up in relentlessly trying to bring out the best in us. As *Friend*, God can be counted upon repeatedly to take us beyond the dependent parent-child relationship and sustain us in higher levels of a more mature relationship with God in which we are God's partners and friends side by side in a mutual undertaking and adventure.

Throughout our lives we need an ongoing relationship with God enabling us to grow and mature, while we are continually being re-parented and launched in new roles, rescued from new

16

dilemmas in order to be empowered for new challenges, and sustained and befriended in new and more mature levels of relationship. We will always need God to be our Parent, Lover, and Friend (some thoughts based upon metaphors for God in Sallie McFague's *Models of God*[4]).

8. **holes in the fuel tank:** God never leaves us stranded when we have gone past the point of no return and the rough road of life has punctured huge holes in the fuel tank of our faith and courage.

9. **"Let go and let God":** This familiar expression "Let go and let God" can be used in a variety of ways to show our need to depend upon God and to forego "do-it-alone" self-help remedies for life's problems and situations.

10. **life's worst and God's best:** Life's *very worst* thrown at us is no match for God's *very best* given to us.

11. **patterns from God:** God can be counted upon to weave new patterns for our lives from the unraveled threads of old patterns of life that have been torn apart by crisis and change.

12. **secure in the palm of God's hand:** It is more likely I can believe God has the *whole world* in his two hands[5] if, first, I can know that at least *my own tiny life* is definitely secure somewhere within the grasp of at least *one* of these huge hands stretching out to close any gap between myself and God.

13. **shelter on the trail:** God provides shelter houses at regular intervals when needed along the roughest wilderness trail that God asks us to travel.

14. **the "love that will not let me go"[6]:** The "love that will not let me go" is, more specifically, God's love that "will not let me go *under*" when, like Peter walking on water (i.e., Matthew 15:30-31), we are in danger of sinking fast and going down, down, way over our heads in big trouble.

C. God's life-transforming power

1. **chess game of life:** Leslie Weatherhead describes the will of God as (1) God's *intentional will* according to God's original "game plan" for our lives, (2) God's *circumstantial will* which goes into effect whenever the original "game plan" must be changed and modified due to changing circumstances in our lives, and (3) God's *ultimate will* which is the final victory when God has the "final say" and the "last word" regarding our lives' outcome and end result.[7] This is to say that God's will is never outmaneuvered by evil's "game plan," because God can make a triumphant follow-up move in our behalf on life's chessboard, no matter what bad moves we have made in playing the game or how badly "checkmated" our strategic situation has become on the game board.

2. **drooping sails:** The wind of God's Spirit can fill our drooping sails and move us ahead, whenever our ship is trapped in the dead, still air of a monotonous, dreary life that is going nowhere.

3. **maximum (divine) vs. minimum (human):** The life-transforming power of God is able to make the divine *maximum* results emerge out of even our *minimum* human possibilities and potential.

4. **rescue mission and rescue operation:** The central theme of the Bible from cover to cover is the story of God's unceasing rescue mission and gigantic scale rescue operation — extending from the very start of human troubles in the Garden of Eden to the final showdown with evil as envisioned in the Book of Revelation.

5. **three dimensional chess game with a fourth dimension:** Our three dimensional existence would be a loser's overwhelming three dimensional chess game if it were not for life's *invisible fourth dimension* in which God is the chessmaster in charge of the outcome of our lives. Because of God's fourth dimension, life is full of amazing mysteries and intriguing puzzles that cannot be grasped by typical simplistic, cynical, three dimensional logic which says 2 and 2 always equal 4, nice guys always finish last[8], and when you're dead you're dead.

18

6. **tiny toeholds:** For every upward climb that looks impossible, God may not provide a quick helicopter ride to the top, but instead gives us *tiny toeholds* for inching our way upward, secure enough for our feet and fertile enough for even the smallest seed of faith to take root and grow quickly.

7. **worth crowing about:** No matter what devastating downfalls and defeats we experience whenever we go all out and try our best to be faithful, there will emerge, through the the grace of God, something of value that cannot be denied to us — an unexpected winner's gold medal for achieving at least a small yet significant victory that is *truly worth crowing about*, instead of nothing but a loser's bittersweet consolation prize for having at least tried our best with absolutely nothing at all to show for it.

II. Language tools in reference to the role of Jesus Christ as our Savior

A. The birth of Jesus, Christmas, and the mystery of the incarnation

1. **alleyway of humility:** Instead of picking a spectacular, proud setting for the birth of a Holy Child, God instead went down past the smelly garbage cans in the dark and narrow alleyway of humility into the back entrance of an old, dingy garage used to house the transportation of guests at an overcrowded, third class hotel.

2. **baby thrown out with the bathwater:** To suggest that we do away with the holiday hoopla and hullabaloo of December by abruptly cancelling all Christmas activity would have to include throwing out the nativity scene and the manger baby, along with the dirty bathwater of all that we object to regarding the hectic holidays.

3. **birth pangs:** Mary's birth pangs were the final labor pains of Israel's history of longsuffering now yielding at last the coming of the long expected Messiah.

4. **charming figurine contributing to arrested spiritual development:** For too many people the child in the manger is just a charming figurine, a rosy-cheeked idol, a baby who never grows up, whose sentimental tug on our heartstrings produces the *infantile paralysis* of arrested spiritual development and diminished spiritual understanding.

5. **Christmas ammunition:** With December's heavy artillery barrage of all kinds of high-powered ammunition erupting furiously and faster than stampeding reindeer, and producing a relentless 24-hour attack of holiday decorations, nativity scenes, Christmas music, Christmas trees, etc., you'd think that people certainly would

get the point of what the meaning of Christmas is all about. But in the war to capture the human soul, artillery is never enough, and it takes a dedicated infantry of foot soldiers to go further door to door, spreading the good news of the Christmas gospel in one-to-one confrontation.

6. **Christmas Derby:** The starting gate opens at the department stores well before Thanksgiving Day, and the reindeer are off and running — the annual Christmas Derby is on.

7. **Christmas truce:** What good is a Christmas truce on a battle-field or in our own embattled daily existence if the Christmas holi-days are regarded as nothing more than just a *temporary escape* from the deadly warfare and the daily treadmill of life from January through November?

8. **driftwood:** The Bethlehem manger, made out of some rough timbers and loose ends thrown together for a child's cradle, is in God's hands an artistic creation of triumphant dimension fashioned out of some scattered pieces of driftwood that had been forsaken and abandoned on the beach in the ebb tide of a lost hope.

9. **elbow room:** God saw to it that in this extremely difficult and impossible world which could be described as an overcrowded hous-ing unit crammed to the rafters with way too many "people prob-lems," there was still enough elbow room in an out-of-the-way animal shelter for the baby Jesus to be born.

10. **Epiphany's wisemen and the world's "wise guys":** In a world too sophisticated to take seriously the simple truth of a child born in a manger back in the days of the great Roman empire, the visi-tors who followed the star from the east were a few authentic, humble *wisemen* in a blasé and blind world dominated by calloused and arrogant *"wise guys."*

11. **faith killed in its infancy:** Today the spirit of Herod is *what-ever* would kill off the spirit of Christmas in its vulnerable infancy

before the infant of our newborn faith can ever have a chance to grow and develop into a mature faith that is a real threat to the powers of evil in our midst.

12. **family encyclopedia:** Like any devoted mother who is the *family encyclopedia* that records in memory all of the events of her children's lives, Mary kept track of all things surrounding the birth, life, death, and resurrection of her son.

13. **ghostwriter for Simeon:** Simeon's *Nunc Dimittis* contains the words of a devout old man who knew his scriptures well and for whom Isaiah is a powerful ghostwriter providing words of inspiration leading Simeon to look at the child Jesus and say, "These words have been fulfilled" (i.e., Luke 2:29-32).

14. **hardboiled humanity:** Despite our modern day sophistication that "knows better" than to be taken in by the compassionate warmth of the Christmas spirit, there is inside us the secret longing for the closing of the enormous gap between our hardboiled humanity and the humble holy child.

15. **helpless handicapped:** We kneel at the manger, helpless and handicapped, feeling hopelessly trapped in our life situations, and feeling so inadequate and unable to give what this unusual child deserves and demands as our total surrender to his claim over our lives. And yet God reaches out to us in our helplessness with a Christmas healing miracle, so that we, like little Amahl,[9] are able to stand and throw away our crutches and return to our daily tasks with a new lease on life.

16. **history's child:** To say that history finds its fulfillment in Jesus Christ is to say that the child in the manger is *history's child* — history's offspring which God as midwife brings out of the labor pains of many centuries.[10]

17. **incarnate love as medicine for the human bloodstream:** The Christmas miracle of God's incarnate love places God in the most

strategic position for meeting our need. Similar to medicine working its way through our human bloodstream until it reaches the strategic point where it is needed, God's incarnate love has worked its way very carefully through all the veins and arteries of Israel's history until at last in the person of Christ such love has finally reached the very heart of all that triggers and governs the pulse and tempo of human life.

18. incarnation — a mystery to Philip and other "blockheads": Philip sounds to Jesus like a befuddled "blockhead" when he says to Jesus in so many words, "You have been with us for so long telling us what God is like, but we ain't seen nothing yet." Jesus' well-known rebuke to Philip, "Have I been with you all this time ..." is similar in some ways to Edgar Bergen's familiar question to Mortimer Snerd: "Mortimer (i.e., you big, lovable, wooden blockhead) *how* can you be so stupid?"[11] Gently but firmly, Jesus rebuked Philip as a "lovable but foolish blockhead" for failing to see that through Jesus we encounter the living God (i.e., John 14:9).

19. incarnation as a "Godsend": There were those who hailed Jesus as a *Godsend* to save them from the clutches of Rome. Little did they realize the deeper meaning of who this "*God*send" really was.

20. incarnation as God's dwelling place: In Christ, God has knocked on the door of our hearts and taken up residence in our innermost dwelling place whenever the doorway to our hearts and our homes is open to God's Holy Spirit. No matter where we live, Christ offers to make our hearts and our homes God's dwelling place.

21. incarnation as God's touching point: Because Christ had the truly human touch in his full and genuine love for people, he was indeed the *touching point* by which the Spirit of God had a full and genuine point of live contact with human life. To be in touch with Jesus is to be *in full touch* with God.

22. **incarnation as the tip of the iceberg:** As the incarnation of *God-with-us*, Jesus is the visible extension of the invisible God, comparable to the visible tip of a huge, invisible iceberg floating beneath the surface of the water. It is the gift of the Holy Spirit entering our hearts that enables us to perceive that, similar to an iceberg, there is definitely in Jesus *something more than what meets the eye* — something invisible and infinitely deeper beneath the visible surface of the human life of Jesus. This iceberg analogy can help to lend credence to the doctrine of the Trinity, in line with what theologian Karl Barth had in mind when he referred to Christ as the Visible Revelation, God as the Invisible Revealer, and the Holy Spirit as Revealedness[12] (i.e., Revealedness understood as God's *capability* via the Holy Spirit to be revealed to us and perceived by us, so that when we see the visible Jesus we are able also to perceive the invisible presence and power of God).

23. **incarnation's key question — "Who do you say that I am?":** The twelve days of Christmas are a time to reflect upon the meaning of Jesus as Emmanuel (God-with-us) and to ponder Jesus' soul-searching question "Who do you say that I am?" (Matthew 16:15).

24. **Joseph as new father:** If something about the Christ child makes us feel awkwardly humble, we can take comfort that Joseph perhaps might have been a typical, flustered new father, wondering what to do at first with a typical, howling infant, before he finally "rose to the occasion."

25. **life's rough and jagged edges:** At Christmas there is a feeling of tenderness that comes to us, so that life with all its rough and jagged edges seems to have a tender touch that is truly amazing and heartwarming.

26. **local nightwatchmen and distinguished V.I.P.s:** Mary was probably astonished that her newborn son was of such compelling interest to some "extreme opposites" who made a point to stop by at the stable — some extremely scruffy-looking, local nightwatchmen and also some elegantly attired, distinguished V.I.P.s from the far east.

27. **long term pregnancy:** The birth of Jesus as the fulfillment of Israel's history gives us hope that, thanks be to God, life for us is not a yo-yo on a string moving up and down and going absolutely nowhere, but instead is best understood as a long term pregnancy which for us will give birth eventually to the best that is yet to be — the fulfillment of our prayers, the fulfillment of our dreams, the fulfillment of our lives.

28. **magnifying glass:** The magnifying glass of the Christmas story lets the penetrating light of God come through so strongly and so intensely in such sharp focus that we are utterly compelled to see life's reality in its truest perspective, as the intense light coming through the glass burns a hole through all our "paper layers" of human ignorance, falsehood, pretence, and pride.

29. **Mary's labor pains and labor of love:** Mary's labor pains in the birth of Jesus were only the beginning of her lifelong labor of love in her son's behalf that took her at last to the foot of the cross.

30. **mountain trail lean-to:** During every twelve-month stretch of our upward climb to reach whatever mountain top happens to be our God-given lifetime goal, we are well advised during Christmastide to put aside our rambunctious ambitions long enough to stop and spend at least twelve days resting and renewing our strength and our spirits in a rough mountain trail lean-to. It may not look like much of a resting place but it gives shelter to a make-shift cradle where a mother takes care of her baby and shares with us the many strange and wonderful things she has been told about this child.

31. **no joy ride or international vacation holiday:** The long trip of the pregnant Mary from Nazareth to Bethlehem was no comfortable joyride, and the flight to Egypt in order to escape the wrath of Herod was no international vacation holiday.

32. **political puppet:** It didn't take much to scare King Herod — just the slightest tug or quick yank on the marionette strings holding

up Herod as the political puppet ruling his satellite country only with the consent and approval of Rome (i.e., Matthew 2:3).

33. **psychedelic red and green:** Our busy Christmas calendar can leave us seemingly lost and stranded, drugged, and addicted in a wildly vivid, red and green, psychedelic fantasy world of *make-believe* — totally out of touch with the reality of what Christmas truly means.

34. **red-faced little tyke:** In contrast to the sweet, cuddly, little Jesus we normally expect to find at Christmas, God's unexpected, surprise gift of a child to us is probably a typical, red-faced little tyke, bellowing away at the top of his lungs in order to be fed, and hugged, and cherished. In fact, some of the greatest artists have painted portraits of "Mother and Child" which no child photographer would ever submit for a "Most Beautiful Baby" picture award.

35. **seniority complex and infant care:** Christmas is a good way to prick the bubble of our adult "seniority complex." If we have reached the adult stage of our lives when we say, "Thank goodness, I no longer have to mess with bottles and diapers and 2:00 a.m. feedings," then it may be a necessary, humbling experience for us to open the door of our hearts and find that God has left a helpless baby on the doorstep, howling for us to take him inside. There are many ways in which the infant Christ appears on our doorstep in the form of someone needing very basic care — a physically challenged person who has suffered a stroke, an elderly adult afflicted with Alzheimer's disease, a whining grandchild in a high chair — but, regardless of "who is at the door," we are called to forego any "privileged character" status we enjoy as adults and "get back to the basics" in simple yet costly loving care.

36. **soft lights of Christmas:** The soft lights of Christmas, coming from a lighted Christmas tree in a quiet, dark room, can bring tears to the eyes and sadness or even terror to the heart when all this overwhelming tenderness makes us remember loved ones who are no longer with us or precious lifelong dreams that have never come

true. In the midst of all this tenderness of a holiday "soft touch" that we generally assume is so comforting and heartwarming, we need to be aware of those lonely persons for whom the powerful sentiment of the Christmas season is a real tear-jerker and for whom a big hug of understanding and compassion is greatly needed and would be most welcome. The soft lights of Christmas may seem way too much for a soft, sensitive part of the heart to handle.

37. **starburst of unexpected light:** If you've ever been rudely awakened by some joker coming into your dark bedroom, snapping on a ceiling light with all its harsh glare, and singing a loud song at the top of his lungs, then imagine how the sleepy shepherds must have felt when a gigantic starburst suddenly shattered the darkness with the blazing brilliance of unexpected light and a huge choir of angels boisterously belted out a "happy birthday" song. Even today Christmas has the capacity to give us a *rude awakening* when we least expect it.

38. **woman in travail:** The Bible utilizes frequently the image of the *woman in travail* to depict the birth pangs, labor pains, and growing pains of the historic process God uses to bring forth fulfillment and redemption.[13] Mary is the "woman in travail" who fulfilled Micah's prophecy that God's appointed ruler would be born in Bethlehem "when she who is in travail has brought forth" (Micah 5:3 RSV). When we consider how parents always die a thousand deaths as they follow with loving concern the ups and downs of their children throughout the years, we would have to believe that throughout the life of Jesus, Mary was always indeed a woman in travail whose lifelong labor of love on behalf of her son was certainly *her labor of love for all of us.*

B. The life and ministry of Jesus yesterday and today

1. **bucket brigade:** The woman at the well had the false impression that Jesus knew how to tap an endless water supply that would put an end to this weary woman's daily bucket brigade (i.e., John 4:11). For many people, like the lonely Samaritan woman at the

well in the heat of the day, life is a weary, one-person bucket brigade every day with no relief from the heat and no friends to offer a helping hand.

2. **coal miner's lantern:** In looking at the foundations of our lives, we need to let the light of Christ shine like a coal miner's lantern taking us deep beneath the ground floor into the darkest depths where we can re-examine the braces, struts, and underpinnings we have trusted to uphold and support the kind of life we have constructed for ourselves.

3. **door:** In St. Paul's Cathedral in London, Holman Hunt's famous painting *The Light of the World*[14] shows Jesus knocking at a very humble door with all kinds of scrubby plants and weeds growing up over it and no handle on the outside. This door opens only when it is opened willingly from the inside by the person whom Jesus is seeking. It is up to us inside to hear the sound of Christ knocking, knocking, knocking persistently at the doorway of the human heart and then to open the door to the Christ who will not use any burglar's methods of forced entry.

4. **fishers of people:** When inviting Simon and Andrew to go fish for people, Jesus surely appealed to the sense of humor of these two down-to-earth fellows. We would hardly expect Simon and Andrew to leave their bread and butter livelihood in order to follow a grimly serious, long-faced preacher and teacher along a monotonous pathway with nothing but saintly stuffiness and sterile goodness as the payoff. To go fish for *people* suggested excitement, adventure, and a challenge even more intriguing than trying to outsmart all the fish in the deep blue sea (i.e., Matthew 4:19; Mark 1:17).

5. **funny money story:** Elton Trueblood's *The Humor of Christ* says that the parable of the unjust steward (i.e., Luke 16:1-9) is told by Jesus in a joking manner.[15] In other words, this parable is a tongue-in-cheek "funny money story" which offers deliberately outrageous, dubious advice to use your money to try to buy your way into heaven.

6. **get a word in edgewise:** The next time you fume and fuss and carry on at great length about "where is God in my godforsaken situation," be aware that there may be a godforsaken-looking stranger beside you with nail scars in the palms of his hands, trying without success to get a word in edgewise.

7. **good for something or good for nothing:** When the wealthy young man said he had followed God's commandments in order to be a good person, Jesus challenged him to follow him and learn how to be "good for *something*" instead of "good for nothing." Jesus said in so many words, "You may be a good guy, but what exactly are you good for?" (i.e., Matthew 19:16-22; Mark 10:17-31; Luke 18:18-30).

8. **highway robbery:** Without ever holding a lethal weapon against anyone's head or heart, Zaccheus and his fellow tax collectors were getting away with "highway robbery, grand larceny, and third degree murder," jacking up the costs of people's taxes in order to make extra money for themselves and their immediate employers (i.e., Luke 18:1-9).

9. **Jesus does not throw his weight around:** In his preaching and teaching, Jesus does not come on "heavy," throwing his authoritative weight around in a "sock it to 'em," somber manner. Instead, he has large crowds eagerly leaning on his every word as he skillfully uses a *light touch* of humor to show that he, the True Authority in the ways of life, is indeed the True Authority in the ways of love (and vice versa).

10. **Jesus the joker:** If we study the picture of Jesus portrayed in Elton Trueblood's *The Humor of Christ*,[16] we get the impression that in much of his preaching and teaching, *Jesus the joker* was having a ball being funny, as he used humorous, exaggerated, ridiculous statements to make his point that the mighty and mysterious ways of God do not always satisfy the strict and overly serious demands of human logic.

11. **merciful friend or merciless manipulator?:** Zaccheus, who shrewdly had taken unfair advantage of his fellow citizens, was indeed fortunate that Jesus was "for real" — truly a *merciful friend* and not a *merciless manipulator*, a clever religious con artist ever ready to cleanse your soul, wash your brains, and clean out your money bags (i.e., Luke 18:1-9).

12. **the Puzzling Puzzler:** Elton Trueblood's *The Humor of Christ*[17] shows that Jesus used puzzles, riddles, and jokes to help people let down their hair and be themselves in the presence of God, as Jesus used his rich sense of humor to help people see that God's love is for real. Yet to many people, including his own disciples, Jesus often was the Puzzling Puzzler whose deeds and behavior were as baffling as his verbal puzzles.

13. **small peanuts:** It perhaps would have been understandable if Jesus, so intent upon going to Jerusalem for the final "big time showdown" between him and his enemies, would never hear amidst the noisy hub-bub of a huge crowd a blind beggar, Bartimaeus, sitting by the roadside crying for help. But Jesus did not have a divided work agenda with one file cabinet marked "big time stuff" and another file cabinet marked "small peanuts." Nobody, including Bartimaeus or you or me, is "small peanuts" in the eyes of Jesus (i.e., Mark 10:46-52).

14. **smartheads:** When Jesus said to the Pharisees, "Why are you putting me to the test, you hypocrites?" (Matthew 22:18), he was addressing a group of *smartheads* who were trying to put Jesus on the spot and make him look ridiculous. Usually Jesus had a way of turning the tables on smartheads, so that *they* were the ones who ended up *smarting* and looking ridiculous.

15. **the "I am —" sayings of Jesus:**
    a. **bread of life:** When Jesus says, "I am the bread of life," he is talking about soul food for our deepest hunger (John 6:48).

    b. **door or gate:** When Jesus says "I am the door" (RSV) or "I am the gate for the sheep" (NRSV), he is saying that his open door policy has no restrictive trade barriers for those who would exchange their old, worn-out patterns of living for the new abundant life Jesus offers (John 10:7).

c. **good shepherd:** When Jesus says, "I am the good shepherd," he is saying that he is the reliable *caretaker* we truly can count upon to be wherever anyone needs to be *taken care of* (John 10:11).

d. **light:** When Jesus says, "I am the light of the world," he is saying that he alone can give us the clear perspective we need to see *where* we should go out in the real world, plus *how to get there* (John 8:12).

e. **resurrection and the life:** When Jesus says, "I *am* the resurrection and the life" (John 11:25), he is saying that right now, *today*, and not just at the end of our earthly life, he can give us new life which springs our captive spirits loose from the paralyzing wrestler's "death stranglehold" exerted by sin and death. These words were spoken to Martha at the time of Lazarus' death. In this way Jesus responded with compassion and vigor to Martha's sorrowful lament that only on a "last day" in the far off future would there ever be a resurrection miracle (i.e., interpretation of John 11:24-26 presented by Paul Hammer, New Testament scholar, at church education workshop).

f. **vine:** When Jesus says, "I am the vine, you are the branches," he makes it clear that nothing less than a living connection to him can keep our spirits vitally alive without becoming dehydrated and dried up (John 15:5).

g. **way, truth, and the life:** When Jesus says, "I am the way, and the truth, and the life," he is saying that when we have *a living connection with him*, he becomes for us (1) the only *highway* that can weave its way through and around our life's many barriers and roadblocks, (2) the indispensable road map

31

showing *the truth* of which highway is actually possible, available, and best for us in spite of the many tempting side roads and detours, and (3) the bountiful blessing and abundant gift of a day by day *life adventure* which makes our journey out on this winding highway with its strange twists and turns nevertheless very worthwhile with Christ as our traveling companion (John 14:6).

16. **the more you learn (about Jesus), perhaps the less you know:** Perhaps Jesus' disciples' difficulty in not being able to see God more clearly through Jesus is due in part to the fact that sometimes "the more you learn, the less you know." In other words, the more you know someone, the more you may realize how much you really don't understand as to *why* this person thinks and talks and feels and acts in a certain way. This may explain to some extent why it was not until after the resurrection that Jesus' disciples finally understood who he was and what he had been trying to communicate to them during his earthly ministry.

17. **truant twelve year old:** At long last Mary and Joseph found their truant twelve year old as cool as a cucumber, sitting in the temple asking all kinds of mind-boggling questions to an astonished group of teachers (i.e., Luke 2:46).

18. **twiddling their thumbs:** One day Jesus kept his mother and brothers twiddling their thumbs outside while he took his sweet time talking to a group of people (i.e., Matthew 12:46; Mark 3:31; Luke 8:19).

19. **upset the apple cart:** When Jesus said, "Do not think that I have come to bring peace on earth" (Matthew 10:34), he was using sharp-cutting, ironic humor[18] to upset the apple cart of those who saw him as only a kindly teacher and a sympathetic healer.

20. **"Who do you say that I am?":** In view of the fact that Jesus often used humor to get across the deepest aspects of his message, it could be possible that it was with *a twinkle in his eye* that Jesus

posed a real brain-teaser and soul-searcher of a question when he asked, "Who do you say that I am?" (Matthew 16:15).

21. **women's lib:** As in the days of the New Testament when Jesus alone showed caring concern for the Samaritan woman at the well (i.e., John 4:7-26) or the Canaanite woman begging for dog's scraps from the table (i.e., Matthew 15:21-28), Jesus continues today to be the only "women's lib" available for many in a masculine-dominated life situation.

22. **yo-yo:** In every sense of the word, Peter was a real *yo-yo* — an up and down, inconsistent, brash big-mouth, who, thanks to endless second chances from Jesus, eventually became Peter, the solid rock, the steadfast leader of the church (i.e., Matthew 16:15-23).

C. The death of Jesus and its meaning

1. **Palm Sunday ride into Jerusalem and the cleansing of the temple:**
   a. **broken branches and crushed flowers:** Perhaps the fragrance arising from broken palm branches and crushed flowers trampled under foot was a penetrating aroma pointing ahead to the sweet smell of victory on Easter after those most crushing, devastating events when Christ had been left on a cross to linger and die like a broken branch and a crushed flower.

   b. **cleansing of the temple:** Just as he drove out the money changers in the Jerusalem temple, so Jesus today would enter the inner sanctuary of our hearts in order to throw out the trash by cleansing us to eliminate whatever shoddy compromises we have made in our relationship to God.

   c. **flowery farce:** We wonder how on Palm Sunday Jesus could stomach this flowery farce of fickle faith, this loud demonstration of love and loyalty that would collapse like a false front in the shadow of the cross. If Jesus is indeed "our precious Savior," it is because human life at its lowest and cheapest level was, nevertheless, precious to him. And so he tolerated both the flowery hosannas and the vicious cries of "Crucify him!" because he had come to cherish and reclaim human life at its lowest and cheapest level.

d. **hosanna:** The hosanna cry of "Save now!" was probably for many no deeper in meaning than our glib television program closing phrase — "God bless you and good night!" For others hosanna was the outcry of fervent faith hoping that somehow the man on the donkey was a "Godsend" who would rescue them from Roman rule. But they didn't understand that this Godsend was truly Emmanuel (God-with-us) sent for a deeper purpose.

e. **let's get it over with:** There are times in our lives when we say, "Let's get it over with," rather than delay any longer with a tough decision. Similarly, when Jesus made up his mind to go to Jerusalem, he had decided, "Let's get it over with!" And so he sent his disciples on ahead to look for the untied donkey, because in every sense of the word, it was high time to get this show on the road toward the final showdown and "get it over with."

f. **morning star:** Although the bright upsurge of hosannas would soon fade away like a meteor shower of falling stars that eventually disappear in the darkness, the ride of Jesus into Jerusalem was a morning star that heralded the triumphant coming of the Easter dawn. The Palm Sunday triumphal procession with its green palm branches proved to be a foretaste and forerunner of the Easter triumph amidst garden greenery.

g. **no hero complex:** Jesus had no "hero complex" leading him to ride on a donkey into Jerusalem, and he knew that many in the Sunday crowd shouting out his praises would eventually join the Friday crowd crying out for his blood.

h. **triumphant entry/entree:** Perhaps it makes greater sense why we describe Jesus' ride into Jerusalem as the "triumphant

entry" when we perceive Jesus to be the "triumphant *entree*."
"Entree" is defined two ways in the dictionary as (1) "freedom
or access to enter" or (2) "the main dish of food at dinner, etc."
Jesus can be described in two ways as the "triumphant entree"
— either as (1) the person who gives people a new "entree" or
open passageway of free access to God's saving love, or as (2)
the person whose sacrifice of body and blood make him, as
symbolized in Holy Communion, the "main entree" of spiritual nourishment available for our salvation.

i. **what a strange ride!:** We have all had the experience of going
on a trip and saying, "What a strange ride!" when the journey
became somewhat "weird and way out." For example, perhaps
the vehicle chosen for the trip was in no way what we expected.
Perhaps strange and astonishing sights and scenery appeared
along the road, or perhaps the road was difficult to navigate with
unusual debris and obtacles in the road hampering our progress.

Similarly, the disciples of Jesus might have thought that
the ride Jesus took on Palm Sunday was a very strange ride —
really "weird and way out." After all, who would expect a donkey to be the chosen "vehicle" for the journey? What a strange
scene with astonishing sights along the road — clothing and
palm branches thrown into the road by a crowd of people shouting their fool heads off! And it must have been extremely slow
traveling for Jesus and the disciples to put up with a homely
little donkey trying to pick its way and forge ahead somehow
through all the scattered debris and rowdy crowd noise.

2. **The Last Supper and later events:**
   a. **Jesus gave of himself at his very best at the Last Supper:**
   In offering his disciples the bread that represented his body
   and the cup that represented his blood, Jesus gave of himself *at
   his very best* at the Last Supper, even though he knew his disciples would be *at their very worst* in deserting him.

   b. **Judas' betrayal:** The kiss of Judas was enough to sicken
   anyone's stomach, and we are forced to decide *whether or not*

Judas is to be pitied as the helpless pawn in a chess game between God and the devil, a puppet on the strings operated by evil forces outside of Judas' control. A crafty defense attorney for Judas would consider whether poor Judas could plead as his excuse — "The devil made me do it!"

c. **last minute bail-out:** Jesus' prayer in Gethsemane was a passionate plea for a last minute bail-out from a flight mission headed for a crash landing. And yet somehow Jesus still had a desire to follow whatever instructions God now would provide, even if the request to "push the eject button" would be denied.

d. **Peter's denial:** When the cock crowed, Peter suddenly realized that he had jumped the gun in bragging that his steadfast loyalty was something worth crowing about.

e. **washing the disciples' feet:** When Jesus got down on his knees to wash the disciples' feet, he showed how God will relinquish all "divine dignity" in order to bend low like a scorned scrubwoman, putting our vaunted pride to shame while ridding our spirits of the most stubborn, highly resistant dirt which only the hands-on, personal touch and the deeply penetrating, cleansing power of God's love can remove.

f. **who is the least among us and who is the greatest:** In Luke's version of the Last Supper, the disciples went on a helter-skelter ego trip that took them quickly from one *grand extreme* to the other. First, they held a frantic "grand jury investigation" to track down who among them was the *least* — "the most lowdown skunk" who would betray Jesus on earth. And next they became embroiled in a "grand lodge fraternal dispute" to pin down exactly who among them was the *greatest* — "the highest level of exalted potentate" who would glorify Jesus in heaven (i.e., Luke 22:23-24).

3. Good Friday and related events:

a. **bail himself out:** One of the two condemned criminals demanded angrily that if the man in the middle had any secret hotline to God, why, oh, why didn't he get on his cellular phone, use his pull and influence to get this execution called off, and bail both himself and the two criminals out of this terrible nightmare (i.e., Luke 23:39). Problem was that the man in the middle was in a situation no less desperate than that of his two Death Row buddies. He was in no way a "politician with top level connections," a "protected son of the Boss or the CEO," or a "privileged character" who somehow could pull off a last minute deal from some "high ranking higher-up" to pry the nails loose and engineer a miraculous rescue operation.

In fact, at one point it seemed to the man in the middle that any existing phone line to heaven had gone completely dead and he had been left literally hanging in a most terrifying and agonizing ordeal, completely stranded and abandoned (i.e., Matthew 27:46, Mark 15:34). But the second of the two condemned felons did not ask for or even expect a "stay of execution." Instead he received from the man in the middle the complete surprise of the unexpected, late breaking, last minute news that the unavoidable cross was, quite amazingly, not the end of the story for this low-down thief and the man in the middle (i.e., Luke 23:40-43).

b. **boiling over:** Instead of boiling over with the angry spirit of retaliation or continually cracking at the seams under the endless pressure of uncontrolled fear and dread, the cup of Jesus' life continued courageously and stubbornly intact, even in the darkest moment of godforsaken despair, as it persistently and constantly overflowed with love, forgiveness, and pity (Luke 23:34). You and I would have been boiling over with rage and bitterness or else "pushing the panic button" if (a) one of our closest friends resorted to a sickening kiss and a phony show of affection in order to let our worst enemies track us down, (2) our so-called friends ran off and left us holding the bag, as a band of hired hoodlums took us into custody, (3) the respectable "powers-that-be" and "pillars of the community" made us go through a shoddy, shameful "kangaroo court" showcase trial followed by the inevitable outcome of an outrageous verdict of "guilty without any established guilt," and (4) a goon squad, skilled in terror and torture, took us into a back room where we were taunted, tormented, and given a brutal going-over.

c. **cheap thrill:** The crucifixion crowd wanted the cheap thrill and grotesque entertainment of legalized murder with a man's life hanging in the balance before their very eyes.

d. **checkerboard game's last move:** Jesus had made his last move on the checkerboard game against the powers of evil and death, and now it was up to God to make the final move via the resurrection that would vindicate his son as the game's triumphant victor.

e. **church gone sour:** We think we would never offer Jesus sour wine to drink, but perhaps he has come to us as a fearful child or a struggling young couple or a lonely old man, and instead of love's sparkling fresh water, we have offered only the sour vinegar of a sour, indifferent attitude. Jesus sees the wasted potential of an indifferent church that has gone sour, and he says, "I am thirsty" (John 19:28).

f. **craziest route to nowhere:** We know what it is to feel perplexed and totally at a loss whenever the family goes for a ride and good old Father insists on driving past the point of no return on the craziest godforsaken route that seems to be leading absolutely nowhere. And so it is understandable that on the cross Jesus became totally baffled and overwhelmingly perplexed by his absurd, crazy, godforsaken journey to wherever God was taking him way past the point of no return (i.e., Matthew 27:46; Mark 15:34).

38

g. **cup overflowing with compassion:** The priceless chalice of Jesus' life always overflowed with precious, merciful compassion for lost souls helplessly trapped on the endless merry-go-round of futility's brutal nightmare. So, therefore, Jesus, high up on the cross, was able, even in extreme agony, to pray for the sleazy crowd of rabble-rousers and horror movie fans who were physically way down below him and also spiritually at the lowest level beneath him, and whose "el cheapo" styrofoam cups now spilled over with merciless scorn and ridicule directed unsparingly toward him (i.e., Luke 23:34).

h. **ebb tide:** As Jesus felt the wane of the pulse of life within him, he knew indeed that the end of life was near and it was time for the ebb tide to take him home to the waiting hands of God, because finally, at last, at last "it is finished" (John 19:30).

i. **execution squad:** For the helmeted execution squad, crucifixion was as commonplace as stepping on a harmless insect or slaughtering and butchering an animal for a holiday feast. But the death of Jesus simply did not conform to the usual expectations of how a crucified man was supposed to die. What had started out for Jesus' executioners as "no big deal" ended up as an earth-shaking nightmare leaving these calloused veterans and their crusty commander completely unraveled and unglued (i.e., Matthew 27:51-54).

j. **fallen leaf underfoot:** In his intense conflict with the giants of evil and death, Jesus did not let his mother Mary become completely ignored and forgotten like a fallen leaf trampled underfoot in the scuffle of battle (i.e., John 19:26-27).

k. **godforsaken loneliness:** Like the mental ordeal of the Vietnam veteran afflicted by violent nightmares linked to a war many say had absolutely no meaning as a completely total waste, the ordeal of Jesus' godforsaken loneliness had reached the critical breaking point of the most terrible and unbearable nightmare where nothing makes sense anymore and everything seems like a total waste (i.e., Matthew 27:46; Mark 15:34).

l. **human horror story:** When we realize that Jesus went all the way in experiencing the very worst, terrifying craziness of the human horror story, we shudder and tremble with gratitude to know that someone has actually gone all the way *through hell* in order to save us from sin and death and set us free.

m. **middle class:** It wasn't the rich or the poor or the sleazy crumbums, but the so-called respectable and responsible middle class "pillars of the community" who arranged for Jesus to be arrested, arraigned, tried, and crucified via clandestine, kangaroo court, legal maneuvers — all part of a quietly orchestrated "white collar crime and cover-up operation" (i.e., Matthew 26:3-5, Mark 14:1-2; Luke 22:2; John 11:45-53).

n. **matador's moment of truth:** As the crowd at a bullfight waits for the moment of truth when either the matador has or has not the courage to lean over the horns of the charging bull and plunge in his sword, so this crucifixion crowd was looking for the moment of truth which would show whether this crucified "King of the Jews" was indeed a courageous King or a cowardly pretender to the throne of courage.

o. **no last minute legal maneuver:** For the three condemned men, there would be no last minute legal maneuver to provide a temporary stay of execution or even a permanent reprieve and a governor's pardon from the hands of Pilate.

p. **noble gesture:** Jesus' offering of forgiveness to his tormentors might seem, at first glance, to be a useless, noble gesture with no apparent impact or impression on the crowd gathered below the cross, but his words of forgiveness reveal the endurance power that enabled his love at its very best to outlast and outdo evil at its very worst (i.e., Luke 23:34).

q. **one of the boys:** To deny that Jesus really felt godforsaken on the cross makes the cross end up as so much pseudo playacting in which Jesus *only seems* to be "one of the boys" caught in the same predicament as the rest of us, sympathizing with us perhaps but yet *not fully* identifying 100 percent with us in our living hell on earth and its godforsaken terror and loneliness.

r. **open air death camp:** They took Jesus up the steep pitch of a hill that had been reserved for human slaughter, an open air death camp known as the place of a skull, Golgotha, and there they stripped him down to his skivvies and strung him up between two scoundrels. If Jesus had had gold fillings in his teeth like many of the Holocaust victims, we can be sure that his death camp executioners would have been quick to grab hold of these sooner or later, but all he had left were his outer garments which were abruptly taken away and raffled off. And in this shameful condition with no outer layer of human dignity remaining, he was the helpless target of public ridicule, plainly labeled in crude, insulting grafitti as "the King of the Jews" with a humilating crown of thorns jammed into his head (i.e., Matthew 27:33-38; Mark 15:22-27; Luke 23:32-38; John 19:16-25).

s. **palm of his hand nailed fast:** They scornfully had nailed a man's hands and feet to a cross, thinking that at long last now they *finally had him* just where they wanted him. But as the long day came to an end, the crowd returned home beating their breasts in holy terror, lamenting and moaning like whipped dogs with heads down and tails dragging between their legs, knowing that somehow and strangely enough it was *they who had been had* (i.e., Luke 23:48). Even though they had nailed Jesus and they thought, "Finally, he's had it!" the truth of the matter is that *it was he who had them!* From start to finish throughout the ordeal of the cross Jesus had the crucifixion crowd securely in the palm of his nailed hand, nailed securely within his unfailing commitment of undying love, unshakeable compassion, and never ceasing forgiveness.

t. **power to puncture people's pride:** If Jesus had simply lived to a ripe old age and died a peaceful, natural death, his death would never have had the power to puncture people's pride or show us just how far we actually will go to crucify goodness whenever goodness fully exposes in a humbling, painful manner just how self-centered we are. If we allow the terrible sight of Jesus on the cross to register its fullest impact within our minds and hearts, the huge nails in Jesus' hands and feet will end up piercing also the thickest layers of our sinful protective armor which has kept us blindly unaware of our deepest need for God's saving grace.

u. **real life horror movie:** The ordeal of Jesus was a real life horror movie with no television commercials to relieve the tension and no "sigh of relief" or speedy Hollywood ending when it's time for the 11 o'clock news.

v. **senseless circles:** As the way of the cross winds its way round and round in senseless circles seemingly going nowhere in the darkness of hell, a voice cries out from the cross, "Why this, my God? Why this?" (i.e., Matthew 27:46; Mark 15:34).

w. **settled cheaply:** Members of the Sunday hosanna crowd found out by Friday that it would be very costly for them to stand by the man they had praised to the skies. Therefore, many settled cheaply with evil and shouted "crucify!" just as they had been told to do.

x. **undergarments:** The typical crucifix may be so familiar to us that perhaps we fail to see that the body of Christ, clad only in the minimum of undergarments, has been stripped of all human dignity and publicly degraded and humiliated in full view of the crucifixion crowd who snickered, hissed, and booed, absolutely relishing and savoring his naked shame.

4. **The meaning of the cross:**
   a. **assertive love:** God's love was *assertive* and not passive in using the cross as God's supreme strategy to break the back of the evil power holding humankind in helpless captivity to sin

42

and death. Instead of being the passive victim of evil's cruelty, Christ was assertive in refusing to give in to the spirit of bitter retaliation and in making the spirit of forgiveness prevail to the very end, eliminating any prerogative or right of evil to claim him through death as the necessary consequence and end result of human sinfulness.

b. **carving out the pattern of the cross:** When we use prayer time or vacation time to stand at a distance from our trials and troubles in order to regain perspective, we will see that God is carving out the pattern of the cross as the pattern for these perplexing life events. Through the grace of God the pattern of the cross is a pattern in which life's hardships and heartaches are painfully forced to add up to something truly worthwhile and significant.

c. **catch the ball and get nailed:** A football player must catch the ball thrown by the quarterback and hold on, even though he knows he will be *nailed* and brought to the ground with a crushing tackle. Even though he knew he would get *nailed to a cross*, Jesus held fast to his faith so that the crushing events of Good Friday would be compelled to yield the Easter triumph. Similarly, we need God's grace to help us concentrate on our own God-given assignment to "catch the ball" and stubbornly hold on, even if we are surely going to "get nailed" when life hits us hard and drops us to the ground. This is what it takes to move forward in the roughest game we have to play.

d. **cross as a symbol of surprise:** The cross has astonishing power as a symbol of unexpected surprise, for it shows life and death in a head-on collision, with life, the unexpected survivor, walking away from the crash.

e. **cross too big to carry:** As followers of the Christ who needed assistance from a passer-by to carry his cross, we too may be given a cross too big to carry. But when God gives us a cross with a challenge too big for us to handle *alone*, God also walks beside us to lend a helping hand so that the cross which would be our "impossible backbreaker" is limited and restricted to bringing out the best in us.

f. **driving nails into the hands of Christ:** In one way or another we all try to stop Christ from reaching too far into our lives and getting "too close for comfort." What this means is that we actually crucify Christ and we drive nails into his hands, as we *try to stop his hands from reaching any further* in order to draw close and make us recognize our need for him. However, our efforts to avoid Christ are in vain whenever we see him nailed to the cross we have created, and we suddenly realize in horror and shame what we have done to him and what our need truly is. No matter how hard we try to nail down the hands of Christ in order to stop him from reaching any further into our lives, we cannot stop Christ from loving us and seeking to reach forth as far as possible in order to reveal the uttermost depths of our innermost need. We may have rejected him and stopped reaching out to him, but *he has never rejected us or stopped reaching out to us*.

g. **finishing touches of an artist's "still life" crucifixion portrait:** People are so familiar with the many, many art gallery portraits of Christ on the cross, that they may be immune or oblivious to the crucifixion's emotional and spiritual impact. Here is a suggestion for an approach in a sermon or discussion group to describe how the crucifixion could be presented to church members as an artist's "still life masterpiece" which can generate a powerful impact and which is given a triumphant dimension from the viewpoint of Easter. This portrait, as described verbally or portrayed on newsprint, etc., could include the following features:

    • the portrait's undercoat and background consisting of *warm, earth tones* applied slowly and patiently as an underlying base coat and foundation representing Christ's down-to-earth love as the *underlying basis* for his sacrifice on the cross;

44

• the *bold brushwork* of a rough-edged cross brashly painted with severe, jagged lines on top of this earth tone undercoat indicating a Christ who is both tough and tender—able to absorb excruciating pain while still continuing to carry out his ministry of compassion;

• some carefully chosen *still life objects*, each with its own silent message regarding the meaning of Holy Week, such as a trampled palm branch, a loaf of broken bread next to a cup of red wine, a crown of thorns, a seamless white robe, a sponge soaked in vinegar, a jagged spear, thirty silver coins with the red stains of blood money paid to Judas, the red feather of the cock that crowed after Peter's third denial, a shiny bowl of water for Pilate's hands stained with guilt;

• the supreme *still life* object that serves as the still life portrait's focal point, center of attention, and finishing touch — Christ's dead body nailed *completely still and motionless* to the cross.

It could be said to our church members that up to this point this still life portrait is at most a pathetic, pitiful picture of goodness completely defeated by evil, love totally held in check by sinful hate, life snuffed out by death, and the still, lifeless, motionless body of a man whose only destination now is a still and silent chamber within a garden tomb. And in the minds of the world's cynics, scoffers, and skeptics, this still life portrait is written off as a sad and sorry commentary regarding a good man's final failure and utter futility. No observer of the grim events of Good Friday saw any hopeful Easter dimension whatsoever on that dark and terrible day. There was absolutely no silver lining observable in the darkest clouds in the sky that day. So an artist could not honestly paint an Easter dimension into the picture itself. An honest and true portrait of the crucifixion would have to be an authentic "still life" with no indication of any hopeful movement or stirring of life or faith.

45

However, we can now point out to our church members that one way the Easter dimension could be added authentically by the artist, as a person with artistic integrity, would be to mount this portrait within a magnificent picture frame adding the Easter dimension as the triumphant "frame of reference" giving the still life portrait of the man on the cross its ultimate meaning and significance. This would be an honest and legitimate step for an artist to take, because a well known, highly treasured, true and complete masterpiece usually is mounted within a magnificent, carefully selected picture frame which in every sense serves as a valuable, essential "frame of reference" bringing out the true depth and dimension of the picture. So because we as Christians believe that the resurrection of Jesus provides the true perspective and the frame of reference for understanding the life, ministry, and death of Jesus, then we can say that the still life portrait of the crucified Christ takes on its full authenticity as an artist's masterpiece when this portrait is mounted within a magnificent and majestic picture frame that provides the Easter dimension of triumphant meaning as the crucifixion scene's true "frame of reference."

As Christians we know that this Holy Week portrait is not a complete and true portrait unless somehow there is also an authentic Easter dimension. Cynics, skeptics, and scoffers are in no position to argue that a majestic picture frame is simply a cheap way to gloss over a gruesome crucifixion scene of suffering and sacrifice. After all, *without* the triumphant dimension of Easter, the events of Good Friday would have been forgotten long ago and never recorded in literature, music, and art. Any still life portrait painted on Good Friday by an on-the-spot traveling artist at the scene of the crucifixion frankly would have been lost and forgotten long ago in history's trash heap of discarded art as just another pathetic and pitiful human scene not worth remembering or preserving. It is very important that we must never forget that the only reason the scene of the crucifixion did not become lost and forgotten long ago and has been preserved in art galleries and in the minds of countless generations down through the ages is because this still life masterpiece has always been framed within the triumphant perspective and dimension of Easter. Again and again we as Christians are called to tell the world's cynics, scoffers, and skeptics whenever they gather in history's art gallery of "remembered great scenes" — "You simply cannot judge the artistic merits or grasp the true artistic meaning of this well known Holy Week still life portrait, until you take sufficient time and effort to see how it is related to its true frame of reference which gives it its Easter dimension."

Because Easter's stunning, magnificent picture frame gives this Holy Week still life portrait its ultimate "frame of reference," its true depth and dimension, and its unforgetable meaning, this still life masterpiece did not get thrown out in history's trash heap, but has inspired the greatest Michaelangelos down through the ages to pay tribute with their talents to the crucified and risen Christ. It is only because the "original scene" on Good Friday took on an Easter dimension that what is now the familiar scene of a man on a cross has been painted again and again by many renowned artists, Gauguin, Rouault, Rubens, etc., and has endured in the world's art galleries as a treasured artistic masterpiece.

h. **harsh medicine:** Not every illness can be doctored with sweet-tasting stuff and easy-to-swallow pills. The cross was the harsh medicine Christ had to take, if we were to be healed from the very worst sickness.

i. **help of the helpless:** The cross and the resurrection show what God's love could accomplish through the seemingly impossible predicament of Jesus *utterly helpless* to spring himself loose. The words "Help of the helpless" from the old hymn "Abide With Me"[19] can give us confidence that just as God did not abandon the helpless Jesus hanging on the cross, so God is also for us in our own most desperate "hang-ups" the readily available "Help of the helpless" — especially when we finally *admit* how helpless we are.

47

j. **high tension wire connection:** Even without the voltage capacity of the electric chair, the cross, nevertheless, enabled Jesus, nailed down and stretched out to the breaking point in his extreme agony, to serve as a *high tension wire connection* between the power of God's love and us. Death proved to be no electrical current resistance barrier that could stand in the way of this love's mighty power surge.

k. **hung up on "the old rugged cross":** We can get so hung up on the schmaltzy sentimentality of "the old rugged cross"[20] that we fail to remember that Jesus hung in agony on the cross in order to deal with *the real hang-ups* that have people trapped in deepest despair.

l. **hunter flushing a partridge into the open:** The cross of Jesus was God's victorious strategy for forcing evil to come out from hiding into the open and become vulnerable to the power of God's love, like a hunter flushing a partridge from the underbrush.

m. **living link and connecting rod:** The ordeal of Jesus on the cross was to be the living link or the connecting rod in *an agonizing tug of war* between God's love pulling in one direction and humankind helplessly caught up in the contrary pull of sin and selfishness in the opposite direction.

n. **murder instincts:** It was not only for people easily labeled as terrible, rotten-to-the core sinners but also for the so-called "nice people," completely blind and oblivious to their cleverly concealed, deeply buried, "murder instincts," that Jesus gave his life on the cross.

o. **power in the blood of the Lamb:** It may be hard for church members to understand the biblical language of sacrifice that speaks of the need "to be sprinkled with the blood" of Christ (i.e., 1 Peter 1:2). However, the meaning of language describing animal sacrifice or the sacrifice of Christ in the Bible can be made more clear (1) by explaining the ancient understanding of how power was released through a sacrificial death, and (2) by making a comparison of this ancient viewpoint to our modern understanding of how power is released through the splitting of the atom.

First of all, church members need to understand that the action of the priest in sacrificing an animal on the altar was seen as an action that released the power of the animal's life as a blessing that brought cleansing and renewal to the people. The *vitality* of the animal was understood to be in the animal's blood, and so sprinkling the blood upon the gathered people was seen as distributing the animal's vitality in a way that brought cleansing and renewal. Similarly, the red wine of Holy Communion symbolizes receiving cleansing and renewal through the blood of the crucified Christ. However, the typical mainline Protestant church member is apt to think that "washed in the blood of the lamb" theology is completely irrelevant and okay for fundamentalists only. And so, it can help to make clear what the ancient biblical language of sacrifice can mean to the modern day Christian, if atomic energy metaphors are used to clarify how the sacrificial death of Christ produces the blessing of cleansing and renewal for us. The sacrificial death of Christ on the cross can be described as "an atom-splitting event" producing a chain reaction release of spiritual power which brings cleansing, healing, and new life.

Like the release of power from the splitting of the atom, so the death of this man, whose hands and feet were split by nails on the cross, released the power of endless life and endless love made known on Easter and producing a chain reaction of redeeming love that has continued across the centuries of human history. This spiritual chain reaction can be described as a continuous, "atom-splitting," ongoing, lifelong sequence both in the life of the church and in the life of the individual Christian. In the life of the church this chain reaction features a dying and rising sequence in which there is continually and repeatedly the death of "the old community of faith" and the resurrection of "the new community of faith." Similarly, the

49

individual Christian experiences throughout life the death of the old self and resurrection of a new self followed repeatedly again by yet another death of old self and another resurrection of new self, and so on.

Furthermore, we can say that this spiritual chain reaction, a dying and rising sequence triggered by the cross and resurrection, has healing power, like cobalt therapy, to heal the cancer of the sinsick soul, so that once again we can freely inhale the life-giving breath of the Holy Spirit. The church and the individual Christian are expected to extend the benefits of this spiritual chain reaction out into the life of the world, so that the healing and life-giving power of redeeming love reaches out to all people everywhere. Through the imagery of atomic energy metaphors, we can help modern day church members to make sense out of the ancient biblical claim that there is indeed "power in the blood of the Lamb."[21]

p. **point of no return for Jesus:** The cross for Jesus was *the point of no return* in his commitment of obedience to God.

q. **shock therapy:** The cross of Jesus stunned the centurion and the crowd as a form of unexpected, high voltage *shock therapy* which triggered their shocking, terrifying realization of *how bad off* they really were in contrast with *how good was the man they crucified.*

r. **spillway:** Christ shedding his blood on the cross was in a real sense a *spillway* sent by God to make the reservoir of God's grace available to us.

s. **the right place at the right time:** The cross is God's strategy for being at the right place at the right time in order to shock us into seeing the terrible truth of our sinful selves, our desperate need for repentance, and our most urgent opportunity to accept God's offer of salvation and forgiveness before it is too late.

t. **way of the cross leads home:** The life of the Christian is a continual sequence of "death and resurrection, death and resurrection, etc." in which our "old self" repeatedly gives way to a "new self" until finally in heaven we reach the ultimate goal of our life's pilgrimage. And so from the perspective of this repeated process of "death and resurrection, death and resurrection, etc." leading to the eventual fulfillment of our lives in God's hands, it, therefore, makes sense to affirm in the words of the old hymn that the "way of the cross *leads home*."[22]

u. **went way too far:** Jesus' enemies decided to get rid of him, because he went way, way too far in revealing unseen, unusual dimensions of the love of God. But where would we be if Jesus had not gone way too far in bringing the healing power of God to us? In his death Jesus reveals the God who always goes way, way too far so that he can get *all the way to the bottom of our human need*.

v. **winter depression hits us in Lent:** Lent is apt to be the season we *put up with* instead of the season we cherish. After all it's a season when we are really fed up with winter. The Lenten cross doesn't exactly appeal to our "escape route" religion instincts that would just love to bypass somehow all the heavy traffic of what we perceive as the church's "somber and serious" Ash Wednesday-Good Friday spiritual pilgrimage. We don't really welcome the idea of joining this pilgrimage and trudging slowly and patiently through the dreary weather of winter and early spring onward toward a hoped for Easter sunrise.

D. The resurrection of Jesus and its meaning

1. **bootstraps:** There is no way the disciples could have pulled themselves up by their own bootstraps out of the darkest depths of their soul-shattering despair over Jesus' death and their overwhelming guilt for having forsaken him. Only the Risen Christ could lift them up through his forgiveness and his assurance that he truly was alive.

2. David's triumph over Goliath in comparison to how Christ's resurrection is victorious over evil: The death of Goliath, the Philistines' "ultimate weapon," terrified the remainder of the Philistine army (i.e., the "lesser warriors") so that they fled for their lives, knowing they were no match at all for David (i.e., 1 Samuel 17:51). Similarly, the resurrection victory of Christ over evil's *ultimate weapon of death* demonstrates his power to prevail over all of the *lesser* weapons in evil's arsenal. This should greatly strengthen our faith and confidence in the power of the Risen Christ to enable us to be "more than conquerors" (Romans 8:37) *in all things great and small.*

3. dead batteries needing a jumpstart: There is no way the grief-stricken, guilt-ridden, and emotionally-drained disciples would have any inner resources sufficient to generate an upsurge of faith, courage, and hope to replace the total despair and the overwhelming devastation they felt after the death of Jesus. The church exists because on Easter the dead batteries of the disciples' drained spiritual energy received a surprise jumpstart as a gift from the risen Christ. The process of the disciples' spiritual uplift and renewal was no quick, short-lived, temporary rejuvenation but was instead a slow, steady recharge that led eventually to the fully power-packed experience of Pentecost.

4. death-and-resurrection chain reaction: Spiritual rebirth and renewal in the life of the individual Christian and in the life of the church result from the continuous death and resurrection process by which again and again the new self replaces the old self and the new community of faith replaces the old community. Over and over again the new self and the new community of faith emerge from the death of the old self and the old community as the result of a repeated "atom-splitting" release of power in a continuous *spiritual chain reaction* extending onward in history from its origin in the death and resurrection of Christ.

5. death pains of the cross became the birth pangs of new life: The biblical understanding of the creative and redemptive power released through suffering indicates that God has the power to change and transform the pains of death into the birth pangs of new life. The miracle of Christ's death and resurrection is that the pains of his death became the labor pains and birth pangs of new and everlasting life. The events of Good Friday and Easter were also the climactic end result of Israel's long suffering history of labor pains throughout many centuries of "learning faithful obedience to God *the hard way.*" Through God's grace the pains of our suffering are transformed into the birth pangs and the labor pains of something new emerging in our lives due to God's great labor of love in our behalf. This renewal process is the repeated death of the old self accompanied always by the birth of a new self, as throughout life we continue to experience the pains of death transformed miraculously into the birth pangs of resurrection.

6. **freedom from our hang-ups:** The empty cross and the Risen Christ are evidence of the power available to free us from all our sinful hang-ups which have had us nailed down in helpless captivity.

7. **gospel for "hard heads":** We can be glad that the Gospel accounts of the resurrection do not try to sugar-coat or minimize the problems that Thomas and other disciples experienced in coping with the surprise of the risen Christ (i.e., John 20:25). Indeed the Easter gospel is a gospel for "hard heads" that has endured throughout history, inspite of all hard-headed efforts to discredit its truth and power.

8. **Paul as the living proof that the risen Christ has power to save us:** We may have difficulty understanding Paul's legal metaphors for how atonement is made to remove the burden of our sin. However, the amazing transformation of Saul, the church's foremost persecutor, into Paul, the church's foremost missionary, is a *living proof* that the risen Christ is indeed able to bring out the very best in us, in spite of who we are at our very worst. Paul proclaimed how Christ continued to save him again and again from being captive to the worst sinful aspects of the "wretched man that I am" (Romans 7:24).

9. **Peter as the living proof Christ is risen:** Peter rose to the greatest *heights* as the leader of the apostles, only because the forgiveness of the Risen Christ had lifted him out of the greatest *depths* of regret and remorse.

10. **picture frame:** The resurrection serves as the picture frame that provides the frame of reference by which all the events of Jesus' life are understood and given their true meaning and significance.

11. **resurrection not a consolation prize:** Life's suffering endured in faithful obedience is not a pointless ordeal or an exercise in futility for which our resurrection then is God's consolation prize given out of divine pity to us to compensate for our "time and trouble." Instead of viewing Easter as the sweet syrup that covers up and compensates for the awful taste of Good Friday's events, we need to see the cross as *a positive accomplishment* with highly essential outcomes and significant results that greatly contribute to the joyful meaning and significance of Easter.

12. **resurrection makes sense only to the crucified:** The miracle of Christ's resurrection makes sense only to people who have been nailed down and crucified. The resurrection miracle in your life comes to you only when you know what it is to be nailed in your tracks and you cry out for deliverance. Perhaps you know the terrible cross of being "stuck on yourself" in your sinful self-centeredness. Perhaps you know what it is to be stuck in your place of daily service because of your suffering love which will not let you cop out and back out of your responsibility to your family, your co-workers, your community, your church, and your God. Anyway, those who want to be lifted up are always those who know they have been nailed down.

13. **stone of disbelief:** The real miracle of Easter is not whether an actual stone was rolled away from the tomb so that the risen Christ could walk out. Instead the real miracle of Easter is that the resurrection of Jesus had the power to roll away the heaviest, most stubborn stone of doubt and disbelief which would have kept the disciples trapped forever in the darkest tomb of despair.

14. **top trump card of evil defeated:** Because death, as the top trump card of evil, was defeated by the crucified and risen Christ, it can be said that Christ has shown he has the power to "take all the remaining tricks" eventually in history's long, drawn-out, high-stakes card game of good vs. evil. Christ's victory over death gives us confidence that he can enable us to prevail sooner or later over all the truly terrible but, nevertheless, *lesser and lower level* trump cards evil has remaining to play. The game's triumphant outcome may be delayed, but through Christ, victory in the game of life will be ours, regardless of whatever cruel maneuvers, hellish heartbreak, or "dirty tricks" evil still has up its sleeve.

III. Language tools in reference to the process of redemption

A. Our human predicament

1. **bills for pills:** When I reach the age when I've got bills, bills, bills, for pills, pills, pills, is there a God who will reach out to me where I am?

2. **bittersweet contradiction:** Nobody ever said life is easy, and it's not easy to live with the perplexing puzzle why life is such a *bittersweet* contradiction of joy and sorrow, light and darkness, love and hate, war and peace, victory and defeat.

3. **"blue heaven" heights or gloomy cellar hole depths:** For some people, "Molly and me and baby makes three happy people in my blue heaven."[23] Yet there are those whose life space exploration has led them not to the heights of a blue heaven filled with joy but instead to the depths of a gloomy, dark cellar hole filled with misery, fear, and despair.

4. **blind spots:** Blind spots are our personal faults that we can't see, but everyone else can, especially our children.

5. **cancer of sin:** Sin is like a cancer which, if unchecked, will bring about a terminal illness leading to the certain death of the soul.

6. **devil made me do it:** Like a drug addict driven by out-of-control compulsions, we perhaps could plead "the devil made me do it" when we fall into what Paul describes as the predicament of being captive to the law of sin, and we end up "doing the very thing I hate" (Romans 7:15). There are times when our enslavement to sin compels us to reject God's hand outstretched to help us, but sooner or later we are held responsible for our decision to

56

grab or reject whatever lifeline God extends to pull us out of the depths of despair.

7. **dumping ground:** Unless we truly care what happens to the elderly, a nursing home can become a dumping ground where pathetic cries and groans are heard up and down the lonely corridors.

8. **frantic merry-go-round:** Many are trapped on the frantic merry-go-round of a life that is going no place with no chance to jump off and start in a new direction.

9. **gambling:** To be naive and unaware about sin's addictive power is like being unaware that the gambling odds are always in the casino's favor and the gambling fever is a compulsive, addictive drive.

10. **hockey goalie's mask:** Similar to a hockey goalie's protective gear, we wear a mask to keep our critics from seeing whether our nerves have had it and whether our feelings have been hurt, whenever the game of life has gotten the best of us and the crowd is jeering at us after the puck has gotten past us into the net.

11. **human ostrich:** I can tell myself and others that I am being patient in finding answers for controversial problems in our society, when actually I am a human ostrich with my head buried in the sand of my own personal safety.

12. **impossible vs. difficult:** We know the frustration of life that leads us to complain to others or even to God — "Why be difficult, when with a little more effort you can be impossible!"

13. **"is that all there is?":** When each morning we stare glumly in the mirror, wondering how we can psych ourselves up to face once again the same old deadly daily routine, the perplexing question of a popular song keeps pounding away again and again at us, like huge ocean waves crashing repeatedly on the rocky shore — "Is that all there is? Is that all there is?"[24]

14. **joy vs. loneliness:** To know yourself as a unique individual can produce the *joy* of "doing your thing," but "doing your thing" sometimes can produce the *loneliness* of being so different from others that very few people can identify with you.

15. **lightswitch:** Worry and anxiety are not something most of us can turn off quickly like a lightswitch. It doesn't take much of a power surge for these two gremlins to make us blow a fuse.

16. **matter of inches:** Only a matter of inches can mean the difference between victory and defeat, or even the difference between life and death. This may be why God asks us to "go the second mile" in our outreach to others.

17. **middle age trap:** The trap of the middle age "sandwich" generation is being caught in the middle between your teenage children and your elderly parents. Your teenagers complain you're always "too close for comfort," allowing them no independent breathing space, while your elderly parents may grumble that you're never close at hand fast enough and often enough when they need you at any hour of the day.

18. **obstacle course:** For many people life is an impossible up and down obstacle course with high hurdles and deep potholes too overwhelming for any amount of human energy to surmount.

19. **our real selves vs. our religious selves:** We may feel like our "real selves" six days a week, but perhaps on Sunday morning at church we feel instead like our "religious Sunday selves." When on Sunday we honestly don't feel like our real selves, is it any wonder that God doesn't seem for real either?

20. **out of gas:** When I have just plumb run out of gas and my drive shaft is broken down and my shock absorbers are completely shot, then, please God, let me trade in this old clunker self of mine that has outlived its usefulness for a new or rebuilt model with increased spiritual horsepower and greater potential to live and serve in the way you want me to.

21. **paperwork and TV:** Is your life boring to the extent that you are in a spellbound trance staring *glassy-eyed* most of the time — either at the mind-boggling paperwork in your office during the day or at the hypnotic television "boob tube" in your family room at night?

22. **point of no return when answers are needed:** When we pass the half-way point of no return between youth and old age, we should realize that we now need urgent *answers* for the soul's survival instead of frivolous *questions* for the mind's amusement.

23. **rigged wheel of fortune:** We wonder at times if life is like a rigged gambler's wheel of fortune with a definite outcome we cannot change, no matter how much we shuffle and re-shuffle the deck life deals to us, or seek out someone we think is the coolest cat or the smartest card shark to be our game partner, or try to persuade the clever wheeler-dealers and the power brokers to put the odds in our favor for a change as we play the game.

24. **rose-colored, stained-glass windows:** Many people have never entered the door of any church, because they see very little light of relevant meaning shining through what they perceive as the naively sentimental, rose-colored tint of the church's stained-glass windows.

25. **runaway planet:** At times we wonder if God or anybody else is really in charge of this runaway planet Earth that seems like a space launch headed out of control on a self-destruct mission.

26. **runaway truck:** Is there any remaining escape ramp for a life that seems headed for self-destruction like a runaway truck with no brakes thundering at top speed downhill on a steep and winding mountain road?

27. **saddest life story:** It is important to build trust with someone so that his/her saddest life story can come out in the open, because this is the only way that healing can come for the deepest hurt.

28. **seniority complex entanglement:** If we get all entangled in a seniority complex — vainly proud of past accomplishments and compulsively possessive of whatever privileges and advantages we have attained — then life becomes an extremely complex maze winding in all directions but leading to a dead end with no new adventure to bring out the best in us.

29. **sixteen tons of responsibility:** There are those who feel they have no life they can call their own when they are stuck with sixteen tons of responsibility and "what do they get, a little bit older and deeper in debt."[25]

30. **smart vs. stupid:** As a frazzled, frustrated parent, I hope I'm at least *half as smart* as my starry-eyed six-year-old brags that I am, but only *half as stupid* as my cynical sixteen-year-old complains that I am![26]

31. **so near and yet so far:** In many ways life can leave us feeling that we are *so near and yet so far* — almost but not quite succeeding in things that truly matter, such as:
   • one more near-miss in trying to smooth carefully and delicately with fine sandpaper the rough edges for two people who always rub each other the wrong way;

   • one more close defeat from someone who always outdoes us in playing bridge or golf, especially if this person never minds telling us with a condescending smile "the error of our ways";

   • one more carefully planned strategy that comes close but doesn't quite succeed for pushing the heavy boulder of a long-existing problem to the top of the steepest hill before once again it slips away and tumbles back to the bottom.[27]

32. **spinning our wheels in the mud:** The more we frantically try to escape from our desperate predicament of being stuck in the mire and mud of evil's many traps by revving the engine and spinning our wheels even harder, while refusing to ask for assistance

60

from God or anyone else, the more the devil delights in our foolish futility.

33. **square peg in round hole:** When your situation at home or at work seems more than you can handle, you wonder how long your nervous system can hold up, like a square peg that just can't fit into the round hole of other people's unrealistic expectations forced upon you.

34. **stale bottle of pop with no fizz:** Life can seem like a stale bottle of pop with no fizz when you're stuck in the same old job or the same old kitchen with no relief from your monotonous mess.

35. **stuck on ourselves:** Being "*stuck on ourselves,*" entrapped by our own self-centeredness, is the worst type of cross to be nailed to. All sinfulness is a version of being "stuck on ourselves," desperately in need of God's grace to set us free from the cross of our self-centeredness where we are helplessly stuck in place and nailed down.

36. **treadmill of routine and responsibility:** Our endless treadmill of continuous, unending routine and responsibility can leave us feeling like a helpless hamster running in a cage utterly godforsaken with no escape hatch for getting free from our vicious circle.

37. **trinity of "me, myself, and I":** Instead of the triune, self-giving God at the center of our lives, the self-seeking god we idolize and adore as the real focal point of our personal worship is often the all-too-familiar, self-centered trinity known as "*me, myself, and I.*"

38. **twisted, awkward position:** Life is always putting a multiple number of extreme expectations upon us, such as — keep your eye on the ball, and your nose to the grindstone, and your foot on the accelerator, and your shoulder to the plow, and your brain working in overdrive, and your blood pressure bursting at the seams, and

somehow in that twisted, awkward, and ridiculously impossible position, now try somehow to get something done.[28]

39. **two pounds:** Two pounds of effort and two pounds of opportunity don't necessarily produce four pounds of satisfaction.

40. **unseaworthy, sinking ship:** People wonder at times if our American society is floundering like an unseaworthy, sinking ship with no reliable captain on board, as they lose confidence in the ability of government, business, education, the church, or any other institution to provide vital leadership and vital answers for navigating the roughest seas we are up against.

41. **upset the apple cart:** As we grow older and become much more vulnerable, it doesn't take very much to upset the flimsy, old apple cart — a broken hip from a fall, or a new arthritis flare-up, or a minor stroke that can prevent even the recall of the name of a friend whom we have known so well for many years.

42. **valley vs. mountaintop:** It's one thing to be way up on the mountain and hear the words of the Sermon on the Mount telling us that we shall be satisfied when we hunger and thirst for righteousness (i.e., Matthew 5:6), but way down in the valley of life's failures, frustration, and futility, we may wonder at times if hungering and thirsting for God's righteousness produces only extreme hunger pangs and an unquenchable thirst, plus no nourishment that truly satisfies.

43. **vicious circle:** Unless the church's outreach of service can relate to the *triple-layered needs* of the individual, the individual's family, and the family's neighborhood or community *all at the same time*, the family gets trapped in the *triple whammy* of a vicious circle in which the individual, the family, and the community only bring out the worst in each other.

44. **whirlpool of despair:** Our grief, without our drawing upon God's help, can only draw us downward into the whirlpool of

destructive despair. Our grief, with God invited to be ever beside us, will become the growing pains that push us upward toward new hope and new life.

45. **yo-yo:** Life's ups and downs can make us wonder if life is just a yo-yo on a string, moving up and down, up and down, and going absolutely nowhere at all.

46. **you and me against the world:** For many households, life is simply a survival game of what the popular song describes as "it's you and me against the world,"[29] with no thought whatsoever of how the family needs to be part of something greater or bigger than itself.

47. **zapped zombie:** Life can become a hypnotic rut in which you slowly become a zapped zombie with no zip or zest.

48. **Zodiac:** In today's space age, there are plenty of stargazers frantically searching for something, studying their daily horoscopes' Zodiac predictions of what to expect if you're born under the sign of Scorpio or Aquarius, and frankly indifferent to the Bethlehem star or whatever dim light filters through the church's stained glass windows.

B. The process by which our human predicament can be redeemed and transformed

1. **blood clots of self-centeredness:** It takes the dissolving power of repentence to break up the blood clots of our ornery self-centeredness that are blocking the main artery of the lifeline between us and God. Christ stands at the door of the human heart, knocking, knocking, knocking in a continued effort to arouse our repentence and obtain our "medical consent" to allow his healing touch to clean out whatever has clogged this most vital artery.

2. **escape hatch religion:** In view of all of the *painless* escape hatch religion that is so popular today, we need to take *great pains*

to spell out what the peace of God really means and how we come to experience this peace, even when there is no escape from our trials and troubles.

3. **fickle favorites:** Unlike the capricious ruler who reserves special "privileged character" status for a few fickle favorites, God extends the privileges of mercy and forgiveness equally and generously to all who sincerely ask.

4. **history not meant to be a meaningless treadmill:** Without God, history could only remain totally under the devil's heavy-handed administration as a meaningless, tortuous treadmill, a cruel and hazardous sweatshop for barely minimal survival, and an endless birth-to-death grind from cradle to casket. But regardless of the devil's plans for our destruction and downfall, God is continually at work to transform or replace the world's dehumanizing treadmills, sweatshops, and daily grinds. Instead of the devil's many vicious circles leading nowhere, God's potter's wheel goes round and round, shaping and reshaping the raw material of human lives into finished and beautiful works of art.

5. **hold them up while we hit them:** Neither tender sympathy nor tough confrontation all alone in isolation from each other are enough to help people grow and change. Instead, in humorous irony, it can be said that our job as a catalyst of change in working with people is to "hold them up while we hit them" — i.e., issuing a tough challenge within a context of affirming a person's self-esteem and self-worth (insight based on statement made by Willis Elliott at church education conference).

6. **hot air balloon:** Whenever we are about to be carried aloft by a balloon filled with the helium or hot air of pride and pretense, it often takes the playful needle of God's grace to puncture enough holes in the balloon to keep our feet on the ground, our heart in the right place, and our head on straight, so that once again we can come to our senses, free to laugh at ourselves and free to live for others.

7. **inner sanctuary of the heart:** Just as Jesus went inside the temple and threw out the money changers, so today he would enter the inner sanctuary of our hearts and cast out whatever is a sleazy compromise on our part in our relationship with God.

8. **jeweled city:** Because God has a vital stake in the outcome of human history, we can dare to dream that our world of smog and filth can become a jeweled city in the midst of a verdant woodland, where the air is fresh, and the water is pure, and every person's skin color is beautiful in the untarnished sunshine, and Love and Peace can be seen holding hands at every street corner and along every mountain stream.

9. **labor of love:** Through God's grace the labor pains of your life will bring forth good things, just as long as your daily efforts are carried out in the spirit of loving-kindness as your lifelong *labor of love.*

10. **lover's quarrel:** Because God is completely fed up with our silent resistance toward God's will, God has started a street corner rumble in a lover's quarrel with a world that God loves enough to pick a fight over.

11. **painkiller given to football player:** God's mercy may actually increase and not decrease our growing pains of realizing why we need his mercy. This is quite unlike the practice of giving a painkiller to a football player so that he can play without the pain of cracked ribs or torn ligaments. God does not want us to risk permanent injury by our being dangerously unaware of where we are really hurting deep inside.

12. **power cables vs. die-hard batteries:** Instead of any ridiculous effort on our part to get an engine to start up when the battery is dead, we need to let God take over and attach the power cables of his mighty love whenever we feel spiritually dead. Even the strongest die-hard batteries of human determination will become dead batteries, if we stubbornly try to lift ourselves up by our own

bootstraps instead of letting God give us the power surge we need to overcome life's troubles and tragedies. It takes God's power hook-up to provide a jumpstart to the dead batteries of our crushed and discouraged spirits.

IV. Language tools in reference to the life of the Christian

A. Prayer and our relationship with God

1. **home:** No matter where the current of life sweeps us, our real home is never left behind, because our real home is in the hand of God. And the hand of God is ever on the move, traveling with God's children throughout all our bright hours of joy and all our dark hours of despair, giving us a "mobile home" that is there for us wherever and whenever we need a refuge of salvation and strength. A magnificent feature of our home in the hand of God is the huge picture window through which we see clearly how our life fits into the widest perspective of God-given meaning and purpose.

2. **island of peace:** Howard Thurman has emphasized the importance of establishing an "island of peace"[30] within our souls where, without pretense or dishonesty or tampering with the truth of ourselves, we bring before God for quiet, unhurried review the purposes and dreams to which our lives are linked.

3. **let it all out, tell it like it is, and let the sunshine in:** A three-step process in deepening our relationship to God is to:
   - *let it all out* — let our real feelings come completely out in the open when we pray;

   - *tell it like it is* — once we've gotten our feelings out in the open, our heads are finally clear enough to recognize the facts of our lives as they really are, so that we now can tell it like it is;

   - *let the sunshine in*[31] — now that the feelings and facts of our lives are out in the open so that we finally can see the forest from the trees, we can now let the sunshine in, as we let the light of God show us the trail through the forest which God has been waiting to show us so that we can move along this trail to the place God wants us to reach.

4. **living contradictions:** As living persons we are "living contradictions," a contradictory mixture of faith and faithlessness, wisdom and foolishness, loyalty and treason, holy commitment and hellish idolatry. As we seek to live in a world of complex contradictions, it can disturb and distress us that our inconsistent and contradictory faith often lacks what it takes to cope with a contradictory world.

5. **noisy distractions and fumbling fingers:** We have difficulty responding to Christ's knock at the door of our heart, when the noisy distractions in our lives make it hard for us to hear the sound of the knock at the door. Also we have trouble working the latch to open the door with our fumbling fingers, due to our *mixed feelings*, making it hard for us to be completely open, completely relaxed, completely honest, and completely obedient to the voice of Christ asking us to open the door.

6. **outsider vs. insider:** It matters greatly whether we have an *outside* or an *inside* relationship with God. The *outsider* is apt to assume that our relationship with God is a matter of meeting God's *minimum* standards of justice so that "I can squeak by and be just good enough to get into heaven." But the *insider* knows from first hand experience that our relationship with God is a matter of God's *maximum* mercy since "there's no way I can ever be good enough to get into heaven." The outsider tries to rationalize whether or not he or she measures up to God's minimum expectations (i.e., by going to church once in a blue moon or contributing occasionally to charity). And the outsider typically makes little or no effort to ask for God's forgiveness or even God's minimum assistance in small matters, but occasionally may want God to show up in a hurry in a time of major crisis. However, the insider freely confesses that he or she has failed God's maximum expectations and urgently requests God's forgiveness and God's maximum assistance to handle even the least of daily life problems and challenges, and not just the big stuff.

7. **oxygen lifeline:** The narrow passageway which Jesus said leads to salvation (i.e., Matthew 7:14) is sometimes like the narrow plastic lifeline feeding oxygen to a patient in intensive care. When we especially need God's intensive care in a time of crisis, we must be extremely careful not to become so uptight with worry and stress that we end up squeezing shut what may be a narrow oxygen supply line as the only way available to link us to the Holy Spirit's breath of new life in an emergency situation. As God's "intensive care patients," it's one thing for us to clasp God's hand firmly as a genuine act of trusting and depending upon him, but it's another thing to clutch so tightly our slim chance of survival in an uptight state of sheer panic that we may end up shutting down God's narrow lifeline extended to us as our only chance for survival in a true state of emergency.

Being human, we naturally tend to fluctuate between prayer and panic, and it's not easy to relax when there's just a slim oxygen tube to depend upon. And yet in order to find salvation's narrow passageway, we need, as best we can, to let go of our most natural, tight-fisted, worrywart, self-centered survival instincts, so that in a spirit of trust we can keep open the indispensable, narrow lifeline through which there can flow freely the peace, power, and joy of a new life that is centered in Christ and not in ourselves. However, since God knows that trust in this type of situation is not easy for us, God's grace makes the most of whatever narrow opening we can muster up in our fluctuation between prayer and panic.

8. **polaroid picture:** There must be enough quiet time spent in prayer, so that, like the polaroid picture that emerges very slowly from the white negative we hold in our hands, there is enough time for the meaning of our relationship to God and the meaning of our lives to emerge slowly and surely from our exposure to the presence of God.

9. **Pueblo Native Americans' spiritual insights:** "... the friars in their long brown robes went around with crossed sticks and prayers and water which they poured on our heads. They told us that we belonged to their religion because they had just baptized us into it.

Some of us mistook these friars for gods. Some of us resisted their religion because we were afraid of it. Some of us were beaten or put to death. In the end we decided it did not make much difference what church there was on the outside. *We have always had a church within ourselves.** This is the one which counts. This is the one which will remain long after all of the outside churches have fallen down."[32] *(italics added)

10. **reservoir, canal, or swamp**[33]: According to Howard Thurman, if you are a *reservoir*, then you are a source of living water that others can draw upon in time of need. If you are a *canal*, then you are a channel through which important things flow between people. However, a *swamp* filled with stale and stagnant water has an inlet but no outlet, and you become a swamp of stale and stagnant water if your *inlet* takes in greedily whatever blessings God would give you, but you have no *outlet* of dedicated service by which you give and share your blessings with others. Your relationship with God should open up both the inlets and outlets in your life, transforming the stale swamp water within your soul into *refreshing well water* suitable to quench the thirst of those you are called to serve. (Thurman's insights were written in an era before the importance of wetlands was recognized, but the analogy of stale and stagnant water still has value for us.)

11. **riding piggyback:** Sooner or later we need to develop our own relationship with God. We cannot continue to be little children riding piggyback on the faith of our parents or grandparents, if we are to become mature and capable to stand on our own two feet in order to handle life's problems and challenges.

12. **take time to be holy:** It is essential, as stated in the old hymn, to "*take time* to be holy."[34] There are no cheap shortcuts, and it takes time to let the light of God's truth probe gradually through the pea soup fog of all our inner confusion, turmoil, and tension, until finally something begins to register, and we realize at long last that God is indeed struggling and striving to get through to us.

70

13. **tide and undertow:** It is best for a swimmer at the seashore to stay away from treacherous undertow currents. However, if the swimmer gets caught in these currents, the worst thing you can do is to struggle against the undertow instead of giving yourself the chance to be carried into the upsurge of a current that can carry the swimmer eventually back up to the surface. Similarly, it is wise to stay away from the tempting allure of sinful situations with undercurrents too much for us to handle. But if we ever find ourselves being swept off our feet by an overpowering, downward tug of temptation, it is both futile and foolish to frantically struggle all alone against the treacherous undertow of terrible temptations and feelings too strong for us to handle by ourselves. Instead we need to ask God to help us get out of the clutches of these temptations and feelings by allowing the prevailing, powerful, incoming tide of God's love to counteract this dangerous downsurge and force the undertow currents to yield us to the upsurge of God's incoming tide.

14. **to each his own:** As the old song says, "to each his own,"[35] and since no one else can live another person's life for him or her, it remains true that to each — his or her own salvation, to each — his or her own cross, and to each — his or her own special gift from God's grace to carry this cross and to work out his or her own salvation.

B. Growing in faith

1. **accelerate uphill or coast downhill:** *Mature* faith is always seeking to accelerate uphill in a lifelong adventure of striving toward the highest and the best, while *immature* faith is satisfied to coast downhill in a lifelong pattern of drifting toward the easy way out. Mature faith *continues to grow* as a blooming perennial plant with its roots in fertile soil or as a living branch connected to the true vine which is Jesus Christ. Immature faith eventually *withers and dies* like a cut flower with no roots or like a dead branch with no living connection to Jesus Christ the true vine.

2. **active listening:** Faith in God often has its beginnings in a nurturing relationship of trust between parent and child or between two friends. One way to build trust is use an "active listening" skill[36] in order to show that we are actively involved in trying to understand someone's real feelings and also that we can be trusted to accept and respect what often are a person's most sensitive feelings. It takes practice to use this skill so that we come across as genuine and not "mechanical" and artificial. However, when we use "active listening" competently as a skill, saying sincerely, "You really feel upset ... discouraged ... scared ... lonely, etc.," we can allow people gradually to sense that they can come out from hiding, present their real selves to us, and also share with God what to them is honestly most real, deep down inside. People flocked to hear Jesus preach, and they put their trust in him because he showed that he truly listened, understood, and cared about people's real feelings. The crowds were indeed eager to listen to Jesus because he showed he was *actively listening* to "where they were coming from" in their spiritual hunger.

3. **"back to the Bible":** Many of those folks who want a sentimental religion that goes "back to the Bible" may fail to realize that the writers of various biblical materials often faced severe personal hardships. If we want to go "back to the Bible," we need to realize that the Bible is neither a sugar-coated cop-out from the "facts of real life" nor a heavenly escape from this cold, cruel world to "the beautiful isle of somewhere."[37] If we don't understand this, then it's too bad we can't travel in a time machine "back to the Bible" and ask the biblical writers what it really was like for them to "live their faith" way back then.

4. **deader than the proverbial door nail:** When God seems far away and faith seems deader than the proverbial door nail, sometimes God asks us to be willing on our part to pry loose one by one all the stubborn nails of unhealthy attitudes, feelings, and habits which may serve to keep the lid on the box containing our dead and dormant faith. This may be a slow process of painful self-examination and self-discovery. But there are no cheap shortcuts by

which a dead and dormant faith can be sprung loose and given new life. God's miracles often include a step by step homework assignment as our part of getting our faith revitalized.

5. **debts like autumn leaves:** Faith may seem easy when money comes easy. But when for the first time in your life, you're really short on cash, and the bills and the debts are piling up faster than autumn leaves falling off the trees, then perhaps we may wonder for the first time in our lives whether there really is a God who stands by us when our own resources are running low and there's more yardwork of leaf raking than we can possibly keep up with.

6. **Devastation Trail:** As I walked the Devastation Trail in Hawaii's Volcanoes National Park, the pathway with the remains of volcanic ash and dead branches on each side was accompanied also by scattered new growth of flowering shrubs springing up. This was a reminder that for those whose life is a sorrowful shambles, God provides a way out — a "devastation trail" with signs of new life emerging out of the rubble to encourage us to keep walking toward something better lying ahead.

7. **ear and eye:** Only through God's grace can I have *an ear* that will not withdraw from hearing the word of God that corrects, admonishes, and challenges me. And only through God's grace can I have *an eye* that is willing to see what for me is truly uncomfortable or painful. For the sights and sounds of life's harshest realities are *too overwhelming and terrifying to handle alone* without God's grace giving us strength, compassion, courage, and confidence to keep our eyes and ears open to what God wants us to see and hear in a world both blind and deaf to the outcry of human need.

8. **faith development imagery based upon insights from Erikson and Fowler:**
   a. **fragile seeds of trust:** In infancy fragile seeds of trust are planted as the young baby's fears and anxieties are relieved by the parent who comes to the rescue of the crying child in order

to make the real world okay again and to show that it's okay to trust and to reach out and to love. The infant's trust in *a loving parent* must be carefully nurtured as the original seeds of the child's later capability to place trust in *a loving God*. Since the first years of a person's life are where trust in God begins, trust in God has its beginnings way back in the seedbeds of the crib and the cradle.[38] When life's tragic events have totally shattered a person's faith in God, it may be necessary to plant slowly and carefully fragile seeds of trust all over again in the seedbed of this person's heart before any more advanced forms of help and reconstruction can do any good. Without the initial or rekindled ability to trust, we cannot move on to greater levels of maturity in our relationship to God and others.

b. **beautiful dreamer:** A young preschool child's use of fantasy shows the childlike quality of the "beautiful dreamer"[39] that should remain with us all our lives. Young children have a rich and vivid imagination of a God who can do all kinds of impossible and beautiful things, just because God is God. No matter what age we are, the "beautiful dreamer" inside us can enable us "to dream the impossible dream"[40] and visualize what are the "impossible" miracles God can bring about to change this world into a better and more beautiful place.[41]

c. **my faith is my life story:** For an elementary school child, "my faith in God is my life story" telling directly or indirectly how God is linked to the events of the child's life. This is the child's own personal *life narrative* which in the child's own words tells "how God, my family, my tree house, my pet hamster, the neighborhood kids, etc., and I" are all part of the unfolding story of the child's daily adventures.[42] For adults as well, their personal faith is always to some degree *their life story* of how God has intervened in their lives from childhood on up. The emotional pull of "my life story" is strong throughout our lives, and this is a key reason why one of everyone's favorite hymns is "I love to tell the story."[43]

74

d. **adolescent search for identity:** The adolescent's search for personal identity results in an effort to declare loyalty to a peer group that provides a sense of "who I am." The church confirmation class has an opportunity to provide the adolescent with a peer group whose sense of "who I am" can be linked to the personal identity and meaning Christ alone can offer. The God who said to Moses, "I am who I am," asks adolescents to discover *who* they are as children made in God's image, so that as a result of extensive searching for true identity, an adolescent at long last can say with conviction and certainty, "I am who I am. I am who God made me to be."[44] Many times during our lifetime, events are apt to happen that stir up doubts and questions about our personal identity, so that we are forced again and again to ask God and ourselves, "Who am I?"

e. **young adult's search for authentic faith:** The young adult's search for intimacy and authentic faith results in an effort to find what can yield a sense of inner contentment and satisfaction — finding "the right person" as a "significant other,"[45] finding a satisfying vocational outlet, and finding a satisfactory personal viewpoint regarding life's meaning and purpose. The church may be perceived as an ally or an obstacle or simply irrelevant in regard to the young adult's effort to establish a personal lifestyle which has a rewarding amount of intimate relationship and a satisfying sense of meaning, direction, and fulfillment. Therefore, the church needs to establish its credibility through a "listening ministry" in places where young adults naturally tend to gather, instead of expecting to lure young adults in large numbers to the church sanctuary's "talking ministry." In our impatience with young adults, we often feel like telling them to "go fly a kite" — which is exactly what God wants them to do, namely, do all kinds of kite flying and launching of trial balloons in the quest of finding out "what is for real."[46] Throughout life, our willingness to "go fly a kite" or send up trial balloons is essential, if we are going to find new answers for life's urgent questions, whenever our familiar approach to life has become shopworn and has outgrown its relevance and usefulness.

75

f. middle-aged adult's desire to be fruitfully productive in spite of life's puzzling ambiguity: The middle-aged adult wants a sense of life accomplishment which more than compensates for the anxiety and frustration of coping with life's many daily puzzles and paradoxes.[47] On one hand, for some middle-agers there can be a sense of overwhelming despair for having passed life's midpoint with greatly diminishing hope of cherished dreams coming true or personal ambitions being realized. On the other hand, a middle-aged adult's most baffling and perplexing life experiences can serve as humble preparation to become receptive to the Christian faith's *paradoxical mystery* of how death is the gateway to resurrection and how God can turn losses into gains, defeat into victory, frustration into fulfillment, and barren failure into fruitful productivity.

As a member of the "sandwich generation," the middle-aged adult often feels "caught in the middle" in a *problems-and-priorities tug of war* between such opposites as (1) home and workplace responsibilities, (2) a continual increase in life responsibilities and a continual decline in physical and mental stamina, plus (3) the testy, touchy relationship with teen-age and young adult children not yet fully emancipated and the increasingly complex caregiver responsibilities in regard to elderly grandparents' increasing dependency needs. Only through God's grace can the middle-age "crunch" of unbearable, ambiguous life circumstances become a "cross" that brings out the very best in the person whom God enables to "roll with the punches" and cope with life's typical middle-age ambiguity of many unanswered questions and no clear-cut immediate outcome in sight.[48] Suitable and welcome nourishment for the middle-aged "sandwich generation" or any adult caught in the double whammy of "crunch and crossfire" should be a priority in the life of the church for those frustrated and exhausted adults who are fed up with lousy tasting "sandwiches."

g. older adult's desire for life's pattern of events to be embraced within God's universal "game plan" for creation: The older adult wants reassurance that his or her life adds up

76

to something that has meaning and value, regardless of the strange twists and turns and detours that the bumpy road of life's journey has taken.[49] This reassurance becomes increasingly important, as the aging process begins to take its toll in physical and/or mental infirmities. To believe in a *future* life after death is strongly dependent upon a *present day sense* of being embraced by God's loving presence and knowing in our hearts that our life pattern is a vitally secure component within God's overall "game plan strategy" through which *the best is yet to be*.

The faith adventure of our older years is to seek diligently and persistently for God to reveal graciously how the up and down, crazy quilt pattern of our lives fits amazingly and triumphantly into God's great game plan for our lives according to God's majestic pattern of *something much greater than ourselves*.[50] When life seems like a dark tunnel, it takes at least one reassuring candle of renewed faith each day to give us confidence that tomorrow and each day yet to come there will be another and yet another lighted candle showing us where to walk forward, so that we can keep moving ahead, expecting to find light at the end of the tunnel. Sometimes you and I are called to be "candles" for persons of all ages who are afraid of the dark and help them find a candle-lit trail indicating how the pathway of a single life fits into God's overall pattern and purpose for us.

9. frivolous adventure vs. do-or-die seriousness: For some adults there may be a time in their lives when it is a joyful *or even frivolous* adventure to chop away playfully at the deadwood of religious traditions and ideas that seem to have outlived their usefulness. But sooner or later life may take on *a do-or-die seriousness* when you feel you no longer can bat around your playful trial balloons and you must find the *elusive, narrow gateway* which alone can lead you to a sense of depth and purpose in your faith and in your life.

10. **going out on a limb:** Like Peter whose courage failed him when he tried to walk on water (i.e., Matthew 14:28-31), we also may fumble and stumble as we go way out on a limb in risking ourselves for the sake of Jesus. But just as Peter gained firsthand knowledge that there is indeed a love that will not let us go under, so we will learn firsthand that even if we falter after leaving the security of "nothing ventured, nothing gained," Jesus is there *for real* when worst comes to worst and we need him in the worst possible way.

11. **Golden Pond:** Senior citizens at Golden Pond[51] will find that a deeper faith is necessary when a quick shift in the winds of life's fortunes can turn the calm waters of Golden Pond into wild waves exposing how vulnerable we are in the later years of life.

12. **gray hairs and nervous stomach:** When children add enormously to parents' gray hairs and nervous stomachs, then parents have to obtain deeper dimensions of faith if they are to find a satisfactory perspective able to see how to weather the wear and tear of childrearing's "aging process."

13. **"give me that old time religion":** Adults looking for a simplified faith to escape from life's *new time* challenges may be absolutely serious but extremely naive when they sing, "Give me that *old time* religion. It's good enough for me!"[52]

14. **kindling wood:** Just as a fire of blazing logs can burn out quickly and unexpectedly unless kindling wood is continually added at the very bottom under the big logs, so even the brightest fire of a living faith will require repeatedly these four pieces of kindling wood in the following exact order as a foundation underneath:
   • the rekindled ability to place our trust in others and God;

   • the rekindled ability to dream the impossible dream and to believe that God has a wonderful dream for our lives;

• the rekindled ability to see the scattered pieces of our lives as our own personal story of what God is doing with the loose ends of our lives;

• the rekindled ability to pledge our loyalty and renew our commitment to the God who wants to take our hand and walk with us on life's journey.

These insights are linked to Erikson's developmental view of personality[53] and Fowler's understanding of faith development[54] which indicate that:

• basic trust gets its start in infancy;

• the capacity for creative fantasy gets its start in the preschool years;

• the capacity to develop "my faith as the story of my my life adventure" gets its start in the elementary school years;

• the capacity to make an informed faith decision to commit my life to Christ gets its start in adolescence.

When Jesus said, "whoever does not receive the (realm) of God as a little child will never enter it" (i.e., Mark 10:15; Luke 18:17), he probably had in mind the type of renewal we need whenever our adult level of faith is getting battered and bogged down, and we need to revisit and rekindle the foundations developed in our early years.

15. **light at the end of the tunnel for the "family lamppost":** The older person who truly knows first hand God's presence and power *need not become overly anxious or apologetic* in regard to being somewhat unfamiliar and out of touch with the newest developments in the real world of the younger generation. What the younger generation needs most from this older person are *not* any detailed, exact answers how actually to construct a new tunnel for moving

forward through the bedrock of a complex new age. Instead of being expected to be a wizard who knows all the important *answers*, this older adult should be called upon to know from the standpoint of practical wisdom and life experience what are the most important *questions* which need to be asked — questions about life's values and priorities that might otherwise get lost and ignored in the darkness.

An older person may or may not have the energy to grab a shovel and join the younger generation in digging a tunnel. However, while other family members dig away in the dark underground through the massive mountain of life's most complex demands and challenges, the older person in vital touch with God's guiding spirit can be the *family lamppost* holding up a light which penetrates the darkness of our uncertainty and confusion in order to point out in sharp focus what are *life's most important questions, priorities, issues, and concerns* that require first and foremost, urgent attention as *very much worth digging into*. Also what is needed from this older generation is the joyful reassurance that there is indeed God's unfailing light at the end of whatever tunnel each generation must dig, so that it is truly worth it to hang in there and keep trying, whenever the digging becomes most difficult and discouraging.

Older adults on close speaking terms with God are in a very strategic position to encourage the younger generation to keep digging away in their lifelong tunnels. First of all, these older adults are near enough to the conclusion of their own lifelong tunnels to see *God's light beginning to appear at the visible end of the tunnel* which they themselves have been digging for many years. Secondly, this older generation is well qualified from personal life experience to serve as the family's inspirational lampposts. The older generation of God's faithful servants can speak from first hand acquaintance with God's trustworthy love and care in order to hold up a strong and steady light of love, wisdom, and encouragement, enabling others to believe that indeed there can be a meaningful sense of *where to proceed* in this lifelong excavation project, and, furthermore, there is definitely something in life's stubborn bedrock *that is worth digging for.*

16. **Little Brown Church:** There are those to whom the word "church" suggests only a sentimental image of the Little Brown Church In The Vale,[55] or a lovely little wedding chapel in a rose garden, or a Christmas card's little white country church in a serene "White Christmas"[56] snow scene. What have we done to help them to take the church more seriously?

17. **little kid's faith:** An adult with a "little kid's faith" perhaps was a child years ago without any adult to help this child's faith to grow. How important it is, therefore, to help adults express whatever level of faith they have without feeling embarrassed or foolish.

18. **loose ends, bits, and pieces:** In order for the puzzling pieces of your life to come together with God's help as a beautiful picture puzzle, you cannot simply dump the loose ends and hard to fit pieces under the table, but instead you must allow God to help you scrutinize all those stubborn bits and pieces which seem to belong nowhere and which defy any speedy solution.

19. **loyalty oath:** The religious right encourages a die-hard loyalty oath of rigid commitment to such hallowed institutions as "the Bible on the table and the flag upon the wall."[57]

20. **mature faith/mature church:** It takes a *mature faith* on the part of church members to produce a *mature church* able to handle its God-given challenges and commitments.

21. **no life to call my own:** When we are caught in the dreary trap of feeling "I have no life to call my own," we need the miracle of God's grace putting joyful meaning and purpose into our lives. The grace of God can arouse within us an awareness that "I now have a life to call my own, because my life now belongs to God and *not* to me alone."

22. **"now I lay me down to sleep":** It can be hard to understand how some adults who are very shrewd in managing their complex

life affairs may have a simple childlike faith that has never grown any deeper than "Now I lay me down to sleep. I pray the Lord my soul to keep."[58] However, for some adults, the more their lives are *way too complicated*, the more they would escape to a faith which is *way too simple*.

23. questions and answers:

a. **buggy questions:** Our religious faith is tested when we have to face life's most troublesome questions that can drive us completely buggy like a swarm of mosquitoes turning life's picnic into a frantic struggle for sanity and survival.

b. **feelings and questions flying like a flock of birds:** The *heights* we reach in our spiritual search for meaning depend upon whether we open up the doors of our innermost selves and let our real feelings and questions *fly upward* like a flock of birds. The journey of personal growth continues whenever a new challenge in our lives stirs up new questions about the meaning and direction of life — new questions flying upwards like a startled flock of birds whose peace and quiet have been shattered by a sudden terrifying noise.

c. **intellectual wise guys:** Some adults become *intellectual wise guys* who take delight in simply questioning and challenging faith's mysterious dimensions, while never paying the price of seeking patiently and persistently the answers that God can reveal only to the open mind and the humble heart.

d. **narrow gate of life's toughest questions:** Life's toughest questions are often the tight squeeze of the *narrow gate* Jesus asks us to pass through before God's answers of abundant life can come to us through the *wide open floodgate* of God's overflowing love.

e. **safe place to ask questions:** Instead of a church that offers "safe, easy answers," we need a church which is a safe place to ask *the most difficult and most painful questions*.

f. **school of hard knocks:** What you really believe is what you have hammered out on the blacksmith's anvil as an apprentice in life's "trade school of hard knocks," as you search persistently for your own answers to life's toughest questions. In life's toughest school of hard knocks, some people flunk the course because they want a faith that provides all kinds of *easy answers* without ever having to face all kinds of *tough questions*. Others pass the course because on the blacksmith's anvil these people have hammered away at life's toughest questions, until with God's help they have hammered out a solid faith which has authentic, profound answers and insights that can measure up to tough times and tough questions.

g. **"Sunday school answers":** When the instructors in life's school of hard knocks start throwing life's toughest questions at you, you'd better come up with replies at a much deeper level than the trite "Sunday school answers" heard again and again in the most boring Sunday school classes.

h. **tangled line inside a fishing reel:** Tough situations can be like a tangled line inside a fishing reel. These complicated situations may force us to face the tough question, "Is this mess really worth untangling?" In response to this tough question, we may be confronted with the tough answer that "Yes, it is absolutely necessary and worth it to untangle this mess, and here is the hard work of untangling that must be done *one knot at a time*." But other times, we are in a situation so hopelessly entangled, that we need to get rid of the tangled fishing line and start all over again and put new line on the reel. This can be difficult to do, when it's hard to give up on all the effort we have invested in salvaging the mess we are in. Neither of these two approaches may be the easy way out for us, and we need God's guidance to give us the proper perspective, plus the persistence, and patience we need.

24. **rabbit's foot:** Animal worship may seem in this modern age to be naive and ridiculous. However, instead of a golden calf, we

perhaps treat God as *the magic rabbit's foot* we need only when we're in big trouble.

25. **second hand faith as a "hand me down":** Perhaps as a child you got by okay with some of the second hand clothes handed down from your older brother or sister, but there is no way you can thrive and survive with a second hand faith which has been handed down to you from your parents or your pastor and which you have never truly reworked and reclaimed as your very own.

26. **senior test pilot:** the older people who mean the most to us are those who truly have earned their wings as "senior test pilot" — those whose success over the years flying in the midst of life's up and down wind currents can give inspiration to the rest of us who may need courage to learn how to fly. As we grow older, our aircraft may become more fragile, frail, and vulnerable to the downdrafts and sudden shifts of wind, but the wind of God's spirit becomes ever more gentle and yet so strong and dependable in lifting the fragile aircraft and its venerable, vulnerable test pilot upward and forward.

27. **spiritual "quick fix":** The uplift of our spirits through God's grace may be more gradual but much more enduring than the temporary relief from a "peace of mind" evangelist's spiritual "quick fix" remedy. A spiritual "quick fix" may temporarily numb our inner pain but not remove its source nor prevent its recurrence.

28. **Superman in disguise:** Everyone knows that meek and mild Clark Kent is really the handsome, dynamic Superman[59] in disguise. Not everyone realizes, however, that even the most outwardly unattractive person has some hidden, *superb*, worthwhile, God-given potential which God is working to develop and make manifestly dynamic.

29. **swinging at bad pitches:** In baseball, even with a count of two strikes, the disciplined hitter will try not to give in to the temptation to swing at bad pitches, and the batter keeps looking for the

good pitch that is worth swinging at. Similarly, our faith is often a waiting game where we learn under pressure to pass up tempting but questionable alternatives, as we wait for a prime opportunity God has yet in store for us.

30. **threadbare level of spiritual maturity:** Spiritual growth requires, first of all, letting go of a threadbare level of spiritual maturity which has outlived its usefulness. Next we need to let God reweave the frayed threads and tattered fabric of our old way of doing things into a new pattern of spiritual maturity better suited for the rugged wear and tear of the greater level of spiritual responsibility God wants to give us.

31. **toe in water before jumping in the lake:** It is often prudent to stick our toe in the water and test the temperature before we jump in the lake of a new adventure. But sometimes faith calls us to "trust and obey for there's no other way"[60] — with neither time nor opportunity to stick our toe in the water prior to a leap of faith.

32. **trial balloons:** There comes a time of decision in our lives when we realize that we can't stand on the ground forever sending up safe trial balloons to dabble with possible options for the meaning and direction of our lives. Instead we have to climb in the basket of a chosen balloon, cut the mooring lines, and trust the wind of God's spirit to take us in a direction that makes our life count for something.

33. **vinegar and baking soda/Americanism:** Vinegar and baking soda are okay separately for household use, but don't mix them together, unless you happen to have a child's toy that is propelled by this specific mixture. Similarly, the ingredients of the Bible, the American flag, apple pie, motherhood, and prayer are okay as separate ingredients, but when you stir these ingredients together into a highly volatile, dogmatic mixture known as *Americanism* or *super patriotism*, you have come up with the extremely bad stuff of a household kitchen concoction that manages to be, believe it or not, as *rigid* as concrete, and yet as *fragile* as glass, and, worst of all, as

rapidly combustible as a short fuse whenever this product is "rubbed the wrong way."

34. **young at heart:** Regardless of our age, the grace of God can keep us young at heart, as God's spirit within us helps us to see life each day as an *adult* entrepreneur's enterprise to be anticipated and cherished with a *child's* sense of adventure and excitement.

C. Facing life and death

1. **artist standing back from the canvas to gain perspective:** We can try to avoid facing the meaning of life and death through the ceaseless activity of one frantic brushstroke after another in painting the picture of our lives. But if we are willing to stop and stand back from the canvas like an artist in search of greater perspective, God will help us to see the pattern of meaning which our brushstrokes are creating. If we let God guide us both when we paint and also when we step back to gain perspective, the pattern of our life's meaning will be a pattern in which all things work together through the grace of God for our good.

2. **barbershop and beauty parlor thoughts and reflections:** A trip to the barbershop or the beauty parlor can be a simple reminder of growing older and facing the meaning of life and death. Gray hairs do come, but, like a skilled barber or beautician, time can make us "better and beautiful" instead of "ornery and sour-looking" — if we place each day of our lives in God's hands. When we ask God to be in charge of each day, then the scissors of time, snipping away at our number of days one by one, are *in God's hands* an instrument of loving care. Instead of a deadly curse, time and the aging process in God's hands become for us a blessing which, like scissors in the hands of a skillful barber or beautician, adds God-given dignity and self-worth by making us look *better* as we grow older, while the number of our days are gradually snipped away.

Older people who have entrusted the days of their lives to God are indeed God's "beautiful people" who through the grace of God look more radiantly alive as time passes. Like the customer with a satisfied feeling from looking into the mirror when the barber or beautician has finished and has performed well, we too can feel like a "new person" when we look in the mirror each day and see a person whose days have been *blessed abundantly* by the craftsmanship and artistry of God's loving, capable hands.

3. **barren rockpile:** When death has taken someone we love, life can seem like a barren rockpile. At such a time the risen Christ comes to reassure us that just as the barren, rocky hill called Golgotha could not prevent the miracle of Easter, so God will transform our barren rockpile into a seedbed where the mosses and lichens of new life have a good bedrock foundation and nothing can stop life's emerging from death.

4. **broken heart/stiff upper lip:** When death has taken someone we love, a broken heart is far better than a stiff upper lip. A broken heart is an *open*, broken-down doorway through which God's comfort and peace can enter, while a stiff upper lip is a tight barricade of stubborn self-reliance that is *closed off* to any outside help. The familiar advice to "let go and let God" is especially appropriate in a time of mourning. When Jesus says, "Blessed are those who mourn" (Matthew 5:4), he is encouraging us to relax the stiff upper lip, *let go* of our painful feelings trapped inside us, and *let God* bring comfort to us through the doorway that is open to God only when our hearts have been broken wide open.

5. **cat with nine lives:** Maybe cats have nine lives, but you and I have only *one* life to live from birth to death, and we are called by God to *make the most* of this one life that God asks us to live.

6. **dead come back to life at quitting time:** A sign at an auto repair service garage reads as follows — "People who don't believe that the dead can come back to life ought to be in this place around quitting time!" Many people have probably witnessed a worker's amazing "miracle of revival and rejuvenation" at the end of the working day. But many people truly find it hard to believe

that there really is a resurrection of the dead when our life comes to an end and indeed for us it's now "quitting time." A lively, dynamic church attracts many people who hope that this vitality is proof that there is indeed a resurrection of the dead we can count upon when life comes to "quitting time."

7. **death is a comma and not a period:** As the story of our life as Christians is being written sentence by sentence, this story eventually reaches the moment of our death but continues onward to be written in heaven as our own portion of "the old, old story of Jesus and his love." Because death is followed by life eternal, we can say that, at the very most, death as *a punctuation mark* in this story is only a *comma* (,) and not a final *period* (.) marking the *end to the story*.[61] As a punctuation mark, a comma is always followed by additional words, and, therefore, a word followed by a comma is never the last word in the story. And so we can sing with joyful confidence the favorite hymn, "I love to tell the story of unseen things above,"[62] a story that gets started on earth and continues onward after death as a story which has no end.

8. **deep roots/shallow roots:** When family roots have sunken deep over the years, it is going to take much more time for the grief and pain of death to be healed. The shallow roots of casual relationships can be torn up without much effort or pain on our part. But the deeper the roots, the deeper the pain whenever someone is taken from us like a tree's roots being torn up from the ground. And yet the greatest comfort and peace from God comes to those whose roots of love have been deep, whose pain is most intense, and whose broken hearts are wide-open doorways God's healing spirit can readily enter. Along with the deep natural roots of natural family relationships torn up at death, there are for God's faithful people the deep spiritual roots that remain intact and which continue to grow and go deep down to tap the most profound resources God makes available in our greatest time of need.

9. **down but not out:** The ordinary view of death is that when you die, you are "down and out." Death for us as Christians is different

in that when we die, we are "down *but not out*," for God will raise us up to life everlasting.

10. **glory road to Glory Land:** We need a twenty-first century vision of the Glory Land to which the glory road leads, if the New Testament vision of heaven is to have any compelling twenty-first century relevance and if church members are going to be convinced that the pilgrimage of faith is indeed *a glory road to somewhere* and not *a sentimental journey to nowhere.*

11. **grief's growing pains:** *Without God,* the pain of our grief can only draw us downward into the whirlpool of destructive despair. *With God beside us,* our grief produces growing pains, as new roots extend downward through our deepest sorrow, establishing contact with the deep level spiritual nourishment that sooner or later causes new green shoots to emerge above in a triumphant celebration of newfound joy.

12. **pattern broken and rewoven:** When the pattern of a family's life has been broken by the death of a family member, God helps us to pick up the broken threads and the loose ends in order to reweave these materials into a new pattern of family life that yields new life and new hope.

13. **suddenness of death like a tree cut down:** Just as it takes very little time with a chain saw to fell a tall tree, so also a human life can be ended very suddenly by death, sometimes when least expected. It is a very humbling experience to gaze at the many rings of annual growth in the stump of a fallen tree, and realize that even the sturdiest tree or the most secure human life is never safe from an unexpected turn of events. Therefore, Christ counsels us to be alert and watchful and ever in touch with his life-giving spirit.

14. **turned-on and tuned-in generation:** We drift aimlessly toward spiritual death when we have become totally *turned off* by our life's daily grind and totally *out of tune and out of touch* with life's most real and vital opportunities for significant adventure.

Instead Christ would get us moving vigorously in exactly the opposite direction leading toward life. He would give us new life by making us his people who are a *turned-on and tuned-in generation* — turned on by a zest for life and tuned in to a two-way frequency wavelength fully and sensitively in touch with both (1) the often unheard voice of human need which only the most sensitive ear can detect and (2) the ever persistent voice of God instructing us how to serve this need in a sensitive, caring way.

D. The cost of discipleship

1. **acid indigestion:** Forgiveness on our part is the best medicine for the acid indigestion of anger, bitterness, and resentment we may feel when we've been taken to the cleaners by people who take excessive advantage of our kindness and generosity. But this means that forgiveness is not cheap medicine and indeed can seem for us like *a mighty tough pill* to swallow.

2. **baptism and Holy Communion:**
   a. **emergency rations/soul food:** The small piece of bread and the tiny glass cup in the communion service remind us that there is always a tiny loophole in the most impossible situation through which God slips us a small dose of emergency rations to tide us over until the dawn of victory emerges from the most awful night of watching and waiting. The small piece of bread and tiny cup are a concentrated, compact form of powerful soul food providing the strongest reassurance that even the smallest seed of God's grace in the soil of the receptive heart will produce an upsurge of new life for us.

   b. **fire baptized:** When you see a store front church with a sign that says "fire baptized," you wonder how many main line churches have members who have been baptized both with water and with the fire of costly and earnest commitment.

   c. **mortal clay transformed into an earthen vessel of divine nourishment:** There is powerful symbolism in the communion service when, instead of a silver plate and a shiny tray of glass cups, earthenware is used for the bread and the wine. In this way we are reminded that in sending Christ to us, God as a skillful potter and artisan has made the mortal clay of Christ's human existence into an earthen vessel fully capable to make the food of divine nourishment readily available to us.

d. **small taste/big bite:** Psalm 34 invites us to "*taste* and see that the Lord is good." Here indeed is kindly encouragement from a compassionate and merciful God who takes into account our fragile and feeble faith which may need *just a small taste* before daring to take a big bite. And so we don't have to be "super saints" who are "truly worthy" to participate in the service of Holy Communion. The small piece of bread and the tiny cup are God's gracious way of inviting all who are "fragile and feeble" to taste and see that the Lord is good. Familiar words of instruction for the service of Holy Communion remind us that we come to this sacred table, not because we are strong but because we are weak and in constant need of God's mercy and God's assurance.[63]

e. **staking a claim:** Just as a miner who has found gold is quick to stake his claim and declare public notice to his rights of ownership, so God, who regards us as more precious than gold, takes timely action to stake a claim to us through the sacrament of baptism which declares to all that we belong to God.

f. **water and the peaceful flight of the dove:** It is interesting to compare that (1) a dove returned to Noah as a peaceful sign after the heavy rains to purify the earth had ended (i.e., Genesis 8:11), and (2) the peace of the Holy Spirit descended upon Jesus like a dove after he arose from the water of baptism with his commitment to God further refined and focused (i.e., Matthew 3:16; Mark 1:10; Luke 3:22; John 1:32). Because God was truly pleased, peace came both to Noah and to Jesus after each in his own way had gone through an experience involving water's power to cleanse and purify. The water in our own baptism symbolizes the complete surrender of our lives to God's purifying love, so that we are made ready for the dove of God's spirit to bring the peace of God's approval.

g. **water from the wells of salvation:** A child's baptism should be a most significant event and definitely not the last time when parents introduce a child to "water from the wells of salvation" (Isaiah 12:3).

3. **brain power/soul power:** It takes a *combination* of brain power and soul power for us to serve Christ faithfully and effectively. This combination involves using *both the left side and right side* of our brains so that our organizing capabilities and our intuitional sensitivity are both in tune with the Holy Spirit's wavelength.

4. **cross too big to carry:** When we become overwhelmed by a cross that is unavoidable and too big to carry alone, we can turn to the Risen Christ to add his grace and his strength in making our burden *his burden* also.

5. **crowded courtroom where our faith goes on trial:** In the crowded courtroom of the real world where our faith goes on trial every day, we may dread being subpoenaed as *a defense witness* sworn to tell the truth, the whole truth, and nothing but the truth, so help us God, in order to render testimony why Christ says we must turn the other cheek, go the second mile, or love our enemies. We'd much rather be *a trial lawyer* with all kinds of clever arguments why we really can't take seriously the hard teachings of Jesus.

6. **dedicated minority:** As the highway we travel in rendering service begins to narrow down from a four lane expressway to a narrow, crummy alley, the travelers decrease in number from a large majority of occasional "do-gooders" to a small dedicated minority of those who persistently hang tough in doing good when the going gets tough.

7. **deserters/draft dodgers/volunteers:** The church is supposed to be a training center for volunteers willing to give their time and

talents to serve human need. In no way is the church intended to be a refuge for deserters and draft dodgers wanting to escape from any involvement in the church's mission out in the world. Just as Jonah ended up in the belly of the big fish as a living nightmare when he tried to avoid the task God wanted him to do (i.e., Jonah 1:17), so the church that refuses to respond to its God-given 911 answering service is asking God to send a whale of a nightmare to evoke repentance, a change of heart, and a change of direction.

8. **diamond-in-the-rough:** It often takes a master diamond cutter a long time to examine a large diamond to see where to cut it in two in order to produce two valuable smaller diamonds (without a false move shattering the larger diamond). Similarly, before we allow ourselves as "diamonds-in-the-rough" to be "cracked open" in a sacrificial act of costly commitment, we need to take enough time to allow the God-given meaning and pattern of our life to become clear enough to indicate exactly what commitment of time and talent God wants us to make. A carefully and "prayerfully" planned action on our part may serve wisely to increase our personal value, while a premature, ill-advised decision could undermine or even ruin our chances to fulfill our God-given, hidden potential.

9. **dying from embarrassment:** The sudden deaths of Ananias and Sapphira in the book of Acts (i.e., Acts 5:1-11) may seem perhaps very strange and unlikely to us, but yet there are people in our present day who cannot face up to the truth of themselves and who would end up *dying from embarrassment* whenever ugly, painful truth points its finger at them.

10. **doormat to a castle:** When do you turn the other cheek, and when instead do you protest over being trampled upon as the convenient but unwilling *doormat to a castle* someone is building at your personal expense?

11. **fishy fish story of Jonah:** Regardless of whether the story of Jonah and the whale sounds like a fishy fish story (i.e., Jonah 1:17—2:10), there's nothing fishy about needing to take seriously this

story's lesson about the cost of trying to run away from what God wants us to do.

12. **fruit is worth the scratches:** There are delicious wild berries which have thorny branches, and we have to decide whether the fruit is worth the unavoidable scratches.

13. **grubby work clothes on Low Sunday:** In the church's earliest years the Sunday after Easter was known as *"Low Sunday"*[64] when new converts resumed wearing their "lowly," ordinary street clothes instead of the white robes they had worn when they were received into the church the night before Easter. We often feel that the Sunday after Easter is a "let down" or a "low Sunday" in comparison with Easter's large congregation decked out in spring finery, but it's time on Low Sunday to put on our grubby work clothes and get back to the lowly, humble tasks of discipleship in the everyday world.

14. **hang together or hang separately:** Benjamin Franklin said to his fellow patriots, "We must all hang together, or assuredly we shall all hang separately."[65] His wisdom can be applied to the life of Christian discipleship, because unless as Christians we hang together in the fellowship of caring and sharing, we will get stung and hung, trying to go it alone.

15. **heart of stone:** The heart of stone is the heart of *stone cold indifference.*

16. **home sweet home:** Abraham had to give up his attachment to "home sweet home" in order to venture forth from Haran, leaving a land of plenty for a *land of promise* (i.e., Genesis 12:1-3).

17. **joy and cost of being a fire knife dancer:** The fire knife dancer at the Hawaiian luau obviously enjoyed putting on a stunning performance, as he rapidly turned and tossed flaming spears of fire. He even added a delightful comic touch, as he would cup his hand to his ear and grin, inviting the audience to cheer his efforts. Later

in talking with him, I asked him if he ever got burned, since nobody is always perfect in performing. He replied that yes, occasionally he did get burned. But this obviously did not take away the joy he experienced in going all out to demonstrate his skill and artistry. It occurred to me that as Christians we should experience the joy of doing our best in serving God, even if sometimes we do get burned as part of the cost of discipleship.

18. **maximum results vs. minimum expectations:** We cannot expect the great surprise of reaching *maximum* results far beyond our expectations if we are content always barely to measure up to whatever *minimum* we know is specifically expected of us.

19. **mission impossible/no consolation prize:** If we go all out in pursuing a worthwhile "mission impossible" but we do not achieve the impossible, God does not then reward us with a consolation prize for our efforts in failing to do the impossible. Instead we receive from God a "gold medal" intended as a first class, first place honor for having stubbornly prevailed in going as far as what was possible.

20. **tapestry woven without shortcuts:** A tapestry illustrating the story of a life well lived has been woven always in a painstaking manner, stitch by stitch, with no cheap shortcuts, and so the end result is a truly magnificent, intricate, and beautiful achievement.

21. **"we almost didn't stop":** We need to remain alert to unexpected adventures God has in store for us. Some of life's unexpected blessings have come when we changed our minds after we first said "no" to turning aside off the main road to look at something that had aroused our curiosity. It may have been a beautiful waterfall or a fascinating gift shop or a heartwarming church service that brought joy to us. And when we got back into our car afterwards, we gave thanks and said, "And just think! We almost didn't stop!"

22. **whistle while we work:** A true test of whether we are truly in touch with the love and joy of Christ is whether we feel in the mood to *"whistle* while we work."[66] If we don't feel like joyfully whistling, humming, or singing while we work (even when silence is mandatory and most necessary!), this can be a clue that we need to be in closer contact with the Christ who deeply desires that "my joy may be in you and *your joy may be complete*" (John 15:11).

23. **world is my oyster:** Residents on Easy Street who think that "the world is my oyster" will never know the sand of suffering and sacrifice which alone can produce a life that ranks in God's estimation as a *pearl of great price*. In order to produce a "pearl of great price" for God, Christians may be called to become *sand in the world's oyster*, a source of irritation to the comfort-oriented Easy Street crowd.

E. The mission of the church

1. **adversary relationship:** The need for cooperation instead of competition in our society is shown in the extremely high costs of the *"adversary relationship"* between management and labor or between lawyers on opposing sides in a court case. The church's mission must be to promote cost-effective *"win-win" approaches to problem-solving*[67] as an alternative to the adversary relationship. The strategy of love is to turn an adversary on the other side of the fence into a partner joining us in a mutual effort.

2. **church suppers should be "Our Savior's Suppers":** Church suppers should be viewed as much, much more than just money raisers or fellowship boosters. In addition to the sanctuary sacrament of Holy Communion, every supper in the church dining hall should also be regarded as "Our Savior's Supper," a special, sacred time when the Risen Christ enters the dining hall, breaks bread, and shares his cup with us as the host at our meal together. Whenever strangers come to enjoy a church supper with us, this could be for them an unexpected sacramental meal where they are blessed

by the Christ who is always looking for an unexpected doorway into the life of a stranger.

3. **Coast Guard rescue ship:** Too many people judge a local church as to whether it measures up to the *comfort standards* of a cruise ship, instead of whether it measures up to the *working standards* of a Coast Guard rescue ship.

4. **drizzle or downpour:** If the church is to help people weather the storms of life, then the church must be able to function in the most annoying drizzle as well as in the most violent downpour.

5. **expectations — ours and God's:** When a congregation is seeking a new pastor, the wrong approach is to find a minister who will measure up to all of *our* greatest expectations and give us exactly *what we want*. The right approach is to ask what are *God's* greatest expectations of our congregation, so that through prayer and self-examination it can be discovered what type of pastoral leadership our congregation *needs*, plus exactly *what God wants* of us.

6. **eye of the hurricane:** Jesus never intended his church to be a ship simply riding out the storms of life in the calm eye of the hurricane. After we have found the peace of Christ in the calm eye at the very center of our life's hurricane, we, as Christ's church, are expected *to head back out into the rough water* where there is a whole world of people in big trouble, and where Christ calls us to lend a helping hand.

7. **homework and workload assignments:** Before the church can "*hit the road*" to carry out its *workload assignments*, it is absolutely essential for church members to "*hit the books*" of the Bible and do some *homework assignments* as advance preparation.

8. **leak in the dike:** Instead of striving to evaluate or improve the entire "flood control system" that society uses to ward off disaster, the church's social action strategy too often is limited to isolated

"do-good" projects for plugging whatever leak in the dike happens to spring loose.

9. **long-winded excuses and gift of gab:** Those who make long-winded excuses why they aren't able to serve in the life of the church certainly have *a gift of gab* that could be used in various volunteer *telephoning assignments.*

10. **lazy river vs. white water rapids:** The church often has to make the choice between traveling *up a lazy river*[68] on a love boat[69] cruise or traveling downstream on a rubber raft *through white water rapids* on a risky mission.

11. **mainstream of life vs. cozy cove:** The church often has to make the choice between risky involvement out in the mainstream of life or secluded isolation in a Back Bay cozy cove.

12. **make this house of God a home:** It takes a while for a family to make a house *a home.* The real test of a church sanctuary is whether this "house of God" has truly become *a spiritual home* where people receive adequate nurture and renewal, and where they truly feel they belong to God and to one another.

13. **mature church and mature faith:** How can a mature church manage to go the distance in its life of service? It requires a congregation of long distance runners with mature faith who can make it at least to the end of the second mile of service where God has set up *the next rally point* to recharge energy needed for the next lap.

14. **nickel and dime crime vs. grand larceny:** The church's social action agenda must include not only the world's most outrageous, cruel, and terrible "grand larceny" felonies as crimes against humanity, but also the "petty larceny" misdemeanors in which the world in all its cleverness knows how to "nickel and dime" a person, stepping on someone's toes just enough to be a real pest without being "bad enough" to justify registering a complaint or a protest. The "nickel and dime crime" is the kind where the victim

would look like a "silly fool" or a "poor sport" and the "court procedures" for getting a public opinion would be too costly, too complex, or too embarrassing, if the victim chose to pursue "such a trivial, minor matter."

15. **Old MacDonald's farm:** Like Old MacDonald's farm,[70] the church can be a busy barnyard crammed with all kinds of programs — here a program, there a program, everywhere a program, program — but does the quality of all this activity match the quantity?

16. **on the spot remedies:** The church's "medical mission" requires us to be *out there* in the real world wherever our Savior is at work healing people's deepest hurts. This requires operating a "mobile medical unit" of skilled "medics" who as a first step feel the pulse of human need and measure the rising temperature out where the fever of violent turmoil is running wild. Their next step is following the exact instructions of Christ's costly prescription or healing procedure for providing love's *on the spot remedies* out on the open pavement where immediate life-saving skills may be urgently needed.

17. **peace in the world:** Peacemaking is essential and imperative. Either we will have *peace* in the world or the world in *pieces*.

18. **pilgrim people:** The church's credentials as a "pilgrim people" can be legitimately linked to its Mayflower heritage, only if today it too is a group of people who leave behind a familiar and comfortable environment, endure the hardships of a difficult journey, and survive the very worst that encounters them in their new surroundings.

19. **plain clothes people:** The police officer who is a "plain-clothesman" wears ordinary clothing instead of a badge and a uniform in order to be more effective in a given assignment. Similarly, the people of the church often are called to be "plain clothes people" whose life of service entails taking the most humble, unobtrusive approach possible without any visible, obvious identifiers of sainthood.

99

20. **precious place:** If the church is to be for people a truly precious place, it must provide a place of *service* as well as a place of *refuge*.

21. **put up or shut up:** A congregation needs either to *put up* the necessary "people power" to do what needs to be done, or else close the door, *shut up* the church, and let someone else who is qualified and eager to get something worthwhile accomplished take over the abandoned building.

22. **reach out and touch someone:** Taking a clue from the telephone company, a church can find a new lease on life by going all out in its evangelism program to *"reach out and touch someone."*[71]

23. **same old four walls:** As we grow older, we may feel confined and tired of staring at *the same old four walls* of our house or apartment or nursing home room. It can make us feel we are part of God's great game plan for everybody if the church can help us to keep in touch with the outside world *beyond* these same old four walls through simple volunteer work for the church and the community — such as phone calls or letter writing, which we can do *where we live* and know it definitely benefits *someone outside our same old four walls*.

24. **six days invisible:** A minister has been defined as someone who is six days invisible and on the seventh day incomprehensible — providing answers to all the questions that nobody is asking.[72] Clergy need to be heard "loud and clear," and be worth seeing and hearing!

25. **sounds of silence and the silent majority:** It doesn't take long for the joyful sounds of celebration to be followed by depressing *sounds of silence*[73] in the life of the church, especially when church attendance is way down on the Sundays after Christmas and Easter. Rather than despair that we in the church are only a "faithful minority," we are called to reach out to the "silent majority," the enormous number of people who are *silently stranded* in isolation

and loneliness. We may be *the only small candle there is* to cast any light whatsoever in the gloomy shadows.

26. **Theory X and Theory Y**[74]: In business management literature, *Theory X* refers to a *dehumanizing management style* which demoralizes and undermines employees by using a rigidly coercive authoritarian approach to implement and enforce company policy and decisions with absolutely no room for substantial employee input, disagreement, or negotiation. *Theory Y* refers to *a humanistic management style* that underscores employees' self-worth by using a flexible, participatory approach to formulate and carry out company policy and decisions with maximum opportunity for worthwhile employee input, disagreement, and negotiation. There are ways in which "X and Y" symbolism could be used in sermons or discussion groups to dramatize the realities of management-employee relations in the world of work.

For example, the irony of how Theory X management operates could be described symbolically as a "letter X" approach in which "X" stands for the overbearing *cross* of inhumane working conditions which management expects employees to accept, no questions asked or allowed. Corporate downsizing in many cases could be described ironically as a *double-cross* operation — (1) laying off employees often without warning or assistance to find new employment, plus also (2) redistributing the work load of laid off employees as an additional burden for those employees who remain on the job. The end result also can be described as a double-cross, if management (1) decides to close up an entire local branch in order to relocate in a Third World country where (2) it can get away with the atrocity of paying its new employees starvation level wages.

On the other hand, a "letter Y" approach to management could be described symbolically as being willing to reach with both arms upward and outward like a "Y" — (1) upward in reaching toward the highest principles of employee relations and (2) outward in reaching out in seemingly opposite directions in order to function as a living, costly link of communication and relationship development between employees who often have diverse or even opposite points of view. Using "letter Y" symbolism, we can say that it always requires *stretching ourselves* upward and outward, whenever we choose to be a "letter Y" person making a vital and constructive difference in the everyday world of work. As a Christian at work I am called to stretch myself upward and outward by going the extra mile in my weekday workplace to improve management-employee relations. My co-workers on Monday have a right to expect this of me, if on Sunday I claim to be a follower of the Christ who on the cross was stretched upward and outward in a "letter Y" effort to bring God and humankind together.

27. **three-legged stool:** Every person has *a three-legged stool* consisting of the individual, the family, and the community as a means of personal life support. The three legs are (1) the *individual's* own inner vitality, strength, and capability to function as a person, (2) the vitality and capability level of this individual's *family* (or another form of immediate support group that gives the individual a primary sense of identity and belonging), and (3) the quality of the life of the surrounding *community* which has impact on this individual and this immediate support group. The seat of the stool represents the individual's "connection" between these three legs, and this "connecting seat" consists of the give-and-take relationship between the individual, the family, and the community. In ministering to individuals or to families or to the wider community, the church must deal with all three stool legs *concurrently and effectively* if there is to be an adequate support system for all concerned. Otherwise the collapse of any one leg means that *the entire stool collapses* with dire results for the individual, the family, and the community.

One main purpose and advantage of this three-legged stool model as a mission education "teaching tool" is to show *why* churches are often ineffective in ministering to an individual or a family or the wider community. It is not unusual for churches to select expediently one easily isolated problem area with a limited, narrow focus exclusively upon either an individual or a family or a community concern. This is to keep in mind only one leg of the three-legged stool without taking into consideration the other two legs. Mission outreach projects become naive, "do-gooder" projects destined to fail whenever there has been no effort to develop *a coordinated strategy* involving (1) individual persons, (2) these individuals' immediate support systems, and (3) these individuals' community networks.

The three-legged stool model can show how each leg contributes to the overall support system or network. Group discussion can focus upon how each leg of the stool can be made stronger and how a vital connection between the three legs can be sustained or improved. The church is called again and again to be a mediator between the individual, the individual's basic support group, and the individual's community in order to help rebuild "broken three-legged stools." This the church must do, if the church is truly serious in its commitment to serve as an effective channel of God's grace in the mainstream of everyday life.

28. **tree planting analogies for the life of a church:** The following "tree planting" illustrations can be used in regard to giving encouragement to a congregation that wants to become more vital:

a. *A tree eventually will bear only good fruit and not bad fruit, regardless of its size, large or small, if it is a sound and healthy tree and is helped to flourish* (i.e., Matthew 7:17-18). A congregation will bear good fruit, if what little assets it has are, nevertheless, sound and healthy and are continually nurtured.

b. *Tree fertilizer in the soil can bring out the best in the tree.* A congregation gets this enrichment through vital Sunday worship, Bible study and prayer, small group activities, worthwhile projects, and active involvement in the wider church fellowship which has resources to offer.

c. *Hard clay needs to be broken up so that tree roots can get needed oxygen and nourishment.* In a congregation the hard clay of rigid and inflexible attitudes and ideas must be broken up in a spirit of sincere penitence if the oxygen of the Holy Spirit is to breathe new life into the congregation.

d. *Tree branches must be pruned which add unnecessary growth and which use energy needed elsewhere.* A congregation must get rid of any unnecessary busywork activities which are a drain on its vitality.

e. *What kind of a tree we have makes all the difference how we care for it.* A congregation needs to have a very clear picture of who it is and what its potential is. This is necessary so that the right amount and type of fertilizer is applied, the soil is in the right condition to nurture the roots, branches are correctly pruned as needed, and there is a definite expectation of what kind of fruit will be produced and what heights the congregation as a "growing tree" will reach. Vague expectations of wanting to be a "growing church" are not enough. A congregation must be *very specific* in its expectations, as there is little margin for error from poor planning and preparation.

29. **tri-focal glasses:** It often takes a considerable adjustment to get used to either bi-focal or tri-focal glasses to correct vision deficiencies. However, *tri-focal vision* is what the church needs to (1) read accurately *at close range* an event or situation immediately happening right under our noses, (2) put this event or situation into its present day context *with middle range vision*, and (3) maintain *a distance vision perspective* to see how this close range event or situation and its present day context fit into a historical long range view of reality. To switch back and forth between these three perspectives may not be easy. However, without this awkward but necessary adjustment to tri-focal vision, the church cannot expect to see accurately what its mission and ministry should be.

30. **trivial pursuit games:** The church needs to center down on what is truly important and forego playing "trivial pursuit"[75] games in pursuing non-essential activities and projects.

31. **trump card of defeat:** Too often in the church it takes only one trump card of disagreement played by an outspoken church member to squelch even the strongest suit of all the talents and

potential existing in the life of the congregation. Since it may take only *one* trump card from the lowest level of our sinful nature to nullify the impact of our virtues and talents, we need to seek out God's grace to bring out the best in us, rather than assume that all our good points outweigh whatever sinful shortcomings we have.

32. **windbreak:** Whenever the strong winds of life's trials and troubles make it hard for a small candle of faith to be lighted, the church needs to serve as a windbreak, providing shelter so that faith has a chance to get started and eventually become strong enough to persist in even the worst storm outside the shelter.

F. Family life and personal relationships

1. **all in the family:** The television show *All in the Family*[76] featuring Archie and Edith Bunker was a humorous yet serious reminder of how many headaches and heartaches families endure rather than resolve, because, after all, it's *"all in the family."*

2. **buddy system/family system:** When I attended Boy Scout summer camp years ago, the *buddy system* used at the swimming area required each swimmer to have a buddy whose hand can be grabbed when the whistle blows for a safety check to make sure that all swimmers can be accounted for. The concept of a "buddy system" is helpful to explain various aspects of family life in connection with what is known as "family system theory."[77]

Family system theory has been used in family counseling to analyze the *overall pattern* of interaction and interrelationship (i.e., *the family system*) that exists within a particular family. It can be said that a family system includes a number of sub-systems or "buddy systems" representing smaller groups of people "holding each other's hands" within the overall larger pattern of the family system. Typical "buddy systems" in the life of a family may include the spouse-spouse relationship, a parent-child or parent-children relationship, a relationship between two or more siblings, or any informal alliance between two or three or more family members. These "buddy systems" can *make or break* the overall family system, depending upon whether they promote healthy or unhealthy relationships between family members.

Family systems theory suggests that *family boundary lines* are important for family members to acknowledge and respect, so that each family member has a definite place in the life of the family with the established territorial boundary lines of "my own private turf" and personal life space ensuring individuality and self-worth. Boundaries between "buddy systems" also are important to respect. Children are *not* to intrude upon the privacy of the special inside relationship (i.e. "buddy system") between spouses. Parents are to *respect* the validity of the special inside relationship (i.e., "buddy system") that exists between the children. Sermons and discussions on family life can borrow insights from family systems theory and focus on themes such as "who is your buddy at home," "who needs a buddy at your house," "the family art of turf-building," "what kind of boundary lines does your family property really need," "good boundaries make good buddies," "your family system — *sick* or *sound*," etc.

3. **crippling circumstances:** "Crippling circumstances" of various kinds can make family life seem impossible and unbearable. For example, the monthly bills are coming in faster than the family income can keep up with them. The kids are exhausting the parents' patience, while the breadwinners' jobs are demanding more and more hours with less time to spend at home. A lengthy illness means long and late hours caring for a loved one with no funds or friends to provide respite relief.

When "crippling circumstances" threaten to immobilize our family and render everyone absolutely useless, the Christ who himself was *completely immobilized*, nailed to the cross, does not abandon us. He seeks to bring his liberating power to bear upon our situation, so that even those "crippling circumstances" we may have to live with (as something not easily or quickly eradicated) yet cannot render us completely helpless and hopeless, totally crippled and immobilized with no constructive alternatives and no triumphant outcome in store for us. The church as the reinvigorated body of Christ is called to provide living proof how Christ today enables the lame to walk and rise above life's "crippling circumstances."

4. **emotional security blanket:** A small child often has a favorite blanket to hold on to for the sake of emotional security. We too may rely on friends or our family or even God to be our emotional security blanket whenever the anxiety of daily living seems too much to handle. Sooner or later a child outgrows the need for a *blanket* as means of security, and turns to other forms of emotional support. Similarly, our dependence upon God and others for emotional support should move beyond the warmth of "complete blanket protection" providing no vulnerable exposure at all to the "cold, cruel world." We need the type of emotional security and support from God that makes us free to take the risks of sacrificial service.

5. **family circus:** Bil Keane's daily newspaper cartoon feature *Family Circus*[78] keeps us aware of the humorous events in family life which make life at home a wacky yet wonderful three ring circus at times.

6. **family feud:** The tradition of the "family feud" has helped to nurture the idea that friction and even violence in the life of the family are inevitable, unavoidable, and can only be tolerated, regardless of whatever deep hurts and traumas may result from all this "feuding and fighting."

7. **house becomes a home:** It takes time for a house to become a *home*, because it takes time to accumulate all the family pictures, it takes time for the attic or basement to overflow with old scrapbooks and keepsakes, and it takes time for the spirit of God to weave together the close-knit relationships of family life amidst all the precious experiences of triumph and tragedy in good years and lean years alike. But no pattern of human life is ever permanent, and, therefore, no home is ever really our "permanent residence." And whenever God has used our human hands to make our house a home and weave together an intricate, closeknit pattern of love in family life, it is hard for us to cope with painful feelings

whenever life at home in a familiar, beloved pattern is disrupted by death or sickness or moving away to a new residence elsewhere.

Whenever a familiar, beloved house can no longer be home anymore due to drastic changes in our lives, God will not abandon us but will help us make the necessary adjustment to a new living arrangement, a new "house" which with God's blessing will sooner or later become *home* to us. In the midst of all of our family's life changes from one living arrangement to another, we can always find a home and feel at home in the hand of God whose steadfast love "puts a roof over our heads" and gives refuge and shelter at all times. And knowing how important it is to feel "safe at home," we need to support very strongly the mission of the church to all homeless persons who have been forced to rely on public shelters or improvised places of refuge.

8. **intake and output valves:** People experience stress and fatigue, whenever they have a *huge output* valve for expending their energy into all kinds of projects and activities, while maintaining a *very tiny intake* valve for receiving new energy and getting re-fueled for the life of service. The enormous output of effort and energy required for family and personal responsibilities must be matched by *a highly effective intake* of the abundant spiritual resources God provides for the abundant output in self-giving that God asks of us. This abundant intake and output are both absolutely essential as the components of the *abundant life* God wants us to live.

9. **salt and spice:** The true life stories that grandparents can tell can have more value and more genuine salt and spice than all the x-rated stories in the supermarket tabloid newspapers.

10. **the more we learn about family members, the less we know about them:** It's true in family life that "the more we learn, the less we know." The more we learn about each other in the family, the less we understand *why* Father always puts on a necktie with a color that never goes with his jacket, or *why* Mother always buys shoes one size too small to look stylish and then complains about

her aching feet, or *why* Aunt Julie always gets the time wrong when she's supposed to show up for dinner, or *why* Uncle George tells the same jokes over and over again. On a more serious level, another family member will always be in some ways *a unique mystery* to us, no matter how long we have known this person. And we need to respect the ways in which God has made each of us *mysteriously unique* with personal qualities and dimensions that may baffle other people but *which are known and cherished by God.*

11. **Transactional Analysis imagery:** The Transactional Analysis (TA) model of personality (based upon neo-Freudian psychology) describes our conscience (i.e., superego) as *the Parent*, our thinking and organizing capacity (i.e., ego) as *the Adult*, and our feeling and emotional capacity (i.e., id) as *the Child*. These three aspects of our personality can function in a healthy or unhealthy manner, and it is possible to use various combinations of metaphors and images to describe these three aspects in terms of healthy and unhealthy functioning. As a resource for preaching and teaching, the TA model should be used only by a professional who has background and training in psychology. The minister with a background in clinical pastoral education or a discussion leader with a professional background in counseling will find it easy to utilize TA's descriptions of the conversations and interactions between Parent, Adult, and Child as a resource for writing sermons or lesson plans. The following examples show how the Parent, the Adult, and the Child can be given "new names" in order to show in simple, down-to-earth language how the interaction between these three aspects of our personality can be *healthy* or *unhealthy*:

a. **Parent:** When the Parent as the custodian of our value system acts in a *healthy* manner to keep us aware of values and priorities to guide our decision making, the Parent can be referred to as *the Nurturing Parent* or *the Good Shepherd.* When the Parent acts in an *unhealthy manner* to browbeat us with an overwhelming rigid conformity to our values and priorities, the Parent can be referred to as *the Nagging Parent* or *the Old Bear.* When the Parent acts in an *unhealthy manner* as neglecting to refer us to any sense of values or priorities, the Parent can be referred to as *the Abdicating Parent* or *the Meek Marshmallow.*

b. **Adult:** When the Adult as our "think tank" plans and organizes in *a healthy, effective manner* which takes into consideration the healthy contributions of the Parent and the Child to our personality, the Adult can be referred to as *the Shrewd Saint* or *the Mind of Christ.* When the Adult as our "think tank" ignores completely the voices of the Parent and the Child and functions in *an unhealthy, headstrong, overly rational manner*, the Adult can be referred to as *the Coldblooded Computer* or *the Win at Any Cost Coach.* When the Adult as our "think tank" is totally at the mercy of the Parent's and Child's demands and functions in *an unhealthy, disorganized, scatterbrained manner*, the Adult can be referred to as *the Loose Screw Lamebrain* or *the Dumb Bunny.*

c. **Child:** When the Child as our reservoir of feelings and emotions functions in *a healthy, playful, constructive manner*, the Child can be referred to as *the Fountain of Youth* or *the Natural Child of God.* When the Child is allowed to run wild in *an unhealthy manner with feelings and emotions completely out of control*, the Child can be referred to as *the Spoiled Brat* or *the Temperamental Tyrant.* When the Child is completely suppressed and allowed *no healthy form of emotional outlet*, the Child can be referred to as *the Bruised and Abused Child* or *the Terrified and Timid Child.*

Healthy dialogue could be portrayed as constructive conversations between (1) the Good Shepherd, the Shrewd Saint, and the Fountain of Youth, or (2) the Nurturing Parent, the Mind of Christ, and the Natural Child of God. There are many possible combinations of *unhealthy dialogue*, such as (1) a vicious guilt-laden conversation between the Old Bear, the Win at Any Cost Coach, and the Bruised and Abused Child, (2) a highly intellectualized and unfeeling approach to life's hardships as expressed in a conversation between the Abdicating Parent, the Coldblooded Computer, and the Terrified and Timid Child, or (3) an out of control outburst of self-centered rage and resentment as expressed in a conversation between the Meek Marshmallow, the Loose Screw Lamebrain, and the Temperamental Tyrant. Sermons and classroom discussions can utilize imaginary dialogues showing the types of healthy and unhealthy conversations that take place inside of us when, for example, (1) the Good Shepherd or the Old Bear is the voice of our Parent as our conscience, (2) the Shrewd Saint or the Coldblooded Computer is the voice of our Adult "think tank" as our mental organizer, or (3) the Natural Child of God or the Temperamental Tyrant is the voice of our Child as our emotional, feeling-level self. The well known Thomas A. Harris' *I'm OK — You're OK: A Practical Guide to Transactional Analysis*[79] and many other TA sources provide plenty of practical, easy-to understand examples showing how the Parent, the Adult, and the Child interact with each other in healthy and unhealthy ways according to the TA personality model. With proper professional guidance, the church's educational program should be able to make competent and easy use of the TA personality model to help adults better understand the inner workings of our conscience, our thinking and organizing capacity, and our feelings.

The Transactional Analysis model of the Adult ego provides a very useful way to describe what it is we Christians are talking about when we refer to *the mind of Christ within us* to guide us in our decision making. In the TA personality model the Adult ego is viewed as an *adult think tank* which handles our planning, organizing, managing, evaluating, and contemplating capabilities. We can say that when we have "the mind of Christ within us," we have through the grace of God an "adult think tank" that plans, organizes, manages, evaluates, and contemplates in the way that God intended. Through the grace of God, our Adult ego as an "adult think tank" can become able to plan, organize, evaluate, choose, and contemplate in a manner that avoids both the heartless, hardnosed style of a *Coldblooded Computer* or the irresponsible, scatterbrained ego style of a *Dumb Bunny*. Furthermore, through the grace of God this Adult ego can review and sort out what are the *legitimate* and *illegitimate* requests and demands of both our *conscience* (i.e., Parent) and our *feelings* (i.e., Child). To have the "mind of Christ" is to endure via God's grace the cross of being willing to function capably in a creative, assertive, *but sometimes painful* tension and tug-of-war directly in the middle between our conscience and our feelings — without succumbing to the temptation to be either a *heartless hardnose* controlled by an overly strict conscience or an *irresponsible scatterbrain* completely at the mercy of compulsive emotional drives.

12. **terrible twos and terrible teens:** A lot has been said about the "terrible twos" as being a very temperamental age for young children and a very trying time for parents. However, with the increased dangers of teen age violence via guns and knives in our high schools, adults are becoming much more alarmed about the out of control behavior of the "terrible teens." Tragically, many so-called "terrible teens" have had emotional and personal problems stemming back to the "terrible two" years and even earlier.

13. **wedding wonderland:** During the Christmas holidays we expect to experience (weather permitting!) the "white Christmas"[80] nostalgia of a "winter wonderland."[81] Similarly, at the time of a wedding there is the expected, traditional "white wedding" and "wedding wonderland" nostalgia complete with white wedding gown, white wedding cake, gifts, flowers, and a getaway car for the newly married couple. Just as some people never get beyond December's "white Christmas" and "winter wonderland" to the deeper meaning of Christmas, so there are those who never get beyond June's "white wedding" magic of a "wedding wonderland" to the deeper meaning of marriage. However, white as the "preferred color" for both the "winter wonderland" and the "wedding wonderland" can symbolize also our wholesome, heartfelt longing at Christmas and at weddings for something pure, clean, and beautiful that can transform our daily "battleship gray" existence.

In Conclusion: Language Skills For A Prophetic Ministry

I hope this book's "clips and quips" not only will provide resources you find useful, but also will serve to spark your own creativity in creating *your own* metaphors, analogies, and language tools. It often is not easy, but it can be fun and even awe-inspiring to take on the very essential task of writing and rewriting as you seek to hammer out your own language tools. Various authorities in the field of religious and theological language can be cited to show the type of challenge we are up against in trying to find suitable language for use in preaching and teaching. In his *Introduction to a Theological Theory of Language*, Gerhard Ebeling stresses that "boredom with language, boredom with words ... (is) ... in a phrase what the present crisis of Christianity consists of, and where its deepest roots are."[82] However, attempts to revise or enliven the use of language in the life of the church today are often at the heart of much controversy, especially in regard to the issue of "inclusive language." Nancy Hardesty disagrees strongly in *Inclusive Language in the Church* with those who complain that creating and using inclusive language is just too much work in order to satisfy a few "fanatics" offended by traditional sexist language. She defends whatever strenuous effort is required in utilizing inclusive language, because "indeed the skills of good writing and persuasive speaking do take work. Using inclusive language is no easier nor more difficult than being grammatically correct or theologically precise."[83]

We should not be at all surprised that we run into difficulties and problems in coming to terms with the language of the Christian faith. Samuel Laechli points out in *The Language of Faith: An Introduction to the Semantic Dilemma of the Early Church* that "the problem of Christian language is as old as the church itself."[84] He cites examples of how the church both in ancient and modern history has had to face the challenge of the friction between the familiar language of faith used *inside* the church and the language developed or borrowed to communicate the Gospel message to those *outside* the church.[85] Randolph Crump Miller emphasizes in *The Language Gap and God: Religious Language and Christian Education* the need for church educators to know how the various language and literary formats in the Bible can be utilized relevantly and skillfully within a classroom conversation which makes use of highly personal,"self-involving language"[86] and the "language of the heart"[87] in a meaningful, rich relationship between teacher and learners. Miller indicates that a dialogue of "self-involving language" between teacher and learners goes significantly deeper beyond matter-of-fact neutrality and objectivity. This language of personal engagement should evoke a genuine, personal response and involvement from the learner and must be related very specifically to the learner's personal "onlook"[88]— namely, how he or she perceives and "looks on" life, the universe, God, etc.

To create new language tools for referring to God may involve us in re-thinking *who* is our God. As Carl Braaten states the case in *Our Naming of God: Problems and Prospects of God-Talk Today*, "changing the language may have the effect of changing the God to whom the language refers."[89] Elizabeth Johnson insists that our language in reference to God does not need to be limited to names for God used in scripture or church tradition. Johnson maintains in *She Who Is: The Mystery of God in Feminist Theological Discourse* that so long as our new words for God "signify something that does characterize the living God mediated through Scripture, tradition, and present faith experience, for example, divine liberating action or self-involving love for the world, then new language can be used with confidence."[90] *In Metaphorical Theology: Models of God in Religious Language*, Sallie McFague indicates that in a theological approach utilizing metaphors and metaphorical models in reference to God, *personal, relational images* are most essential for describing who God is, such as father, mother, lover, friend, savior, ruler, governor, servant, companion, comrade, liberator, etc. Therefore, in our manner of describing and referring to God "*many* metaphors and models are necessary ... (and) ... a piling up of images is essential, both to avoid idolatry and to attempt to express the richness and variety of the divine-human relationship."[91]

So with boldness let us proceed to develop new and improved language tools, knowing that "it ain't easy" and realizing that in this painstaking process we may find many, many new ways of referring to God, plus a new awareness of *who* God is for us. Often it has been said that we are called to a "prophetic ministry" as pastors and teachers. Regardless of how we define "prophetic ministry," we would do well to keep in mind how the biblical prophet's "ministerial role" included the prophet's skillful and inspired use of well chosen words and images. If we study the words of the prophets in the Bible, we will find that the prophets were very adept in their use of language tools to make their message come alive. The prophet was called by God to "tell it like it is" and to use dramatic "show and tell" imagery so that people could *see* as well as hear how God made a difference in their lives.

The prophet Ezekiel's imaginative use of language tools serves as a lively, colorful model of what "prophetic ministry" at its best can be. Granted, Ezekiel's powerful imagery may seem at times really wild and way out — for example, as expressed in the words of the familiar spiritual — "a wheel within a wheel way in the middle of the air"[92] (i.e., Ezekiel 10:10). However, as "modern day Ezekiels," we need to let our own imaginations run *wild* and come up with lively images which put *"little wheels"* within the "big wheels" of major biblical themes — i.e., the "little wheels" of metaphors, analogies, and language tools which, somehow like a set of connecting gears inside a machine, serve to help the "big wheel" begin to move s-l-o-w-l-y but surely in our minds until — suddenly the "big wheel" of the major biblical theme (such as "grace," "atonement," "salvation," etc.) moves off dead center and begins to make sense to us as something dynamic and vital.

Just for fun, let us now use our imaginations to see how Ezekiel and his vivid visions could serve as a helpful source of encouragement to the frazzled preacher or the desperate teacher struggling to cope with theological or biblical material that may seem extremely difficult to present in a lively, relevant manner. For example, let us suppose that you follow the lectionary in selecting your sermon or class themes, and although this discipline usually seems fruitful and rewarding, there are times when a particular lectionary text

115

simply leaves you completely cold and unenthusiastic. Anyway, allow yourself to imagine that you are faced with a lectionary passage which seems somewhat obscure in meaning, or lacking in any immediately obvious relevance, or, frankly, just plain boring and uninspiring! And you ask yourself (and God), "how in the world am I ever going to use *that* as the basis of a lively and helpful sermon or class discussion?" But yet perhaps there is something about this lectionary text that will not let you just give up and try working with another scriptural passsage. At such a time you certainly may feel like the prophet Ezekiel, stranded in the middle of a valley full of dry bones (i.e., Ezekiel 37:1), as you struggle with a lectionary text that seems "duller than doughnuts and deader than a door nail!" (to cite the familiar woebegone words of lament!)

As you stare at this "terrible text," while the crumpled up papers of your sermon or your church school lesson manuscripts lay scattered across the floor like bones scattered across a desolate valley, the words of this difficult lectionary text may seem indeed like dry, useless bones with absolutely no life to them. And now in this moment of deep level exasperation, let us imagine that a voice comes to you as it came to Ezekiel saying, *"Mortal, can these bones live?"* (Ezekiel 37:3a). Truly such words might sound at first like a terribly bad joke, adding insult to injury, especially whenever your creative juices have been squeezed dry, and there is very little time left before your Sunday morning deadline!

At this point your anxiety and frustration could understandably reach the breaking point, and yet, like Ezekiel, you might react to the question, "Can these bones live?" in a spirit of hopeful trust by responding either verbally or non-verbally, *"O Great God, you know"* (i.e., Ezekiel 37:3b in a manner using inclusive language)! But with your eleventh hour deadline rapidly closing in, you also might really explode and lose your cool completely, and instead you mumble and grumble angrily, "O God only knows *why* somebody picked this terrible text!" So what is most crucial at this point is whether our cry of angry frustration, "God only knows!" becomes mingled with or followed by a cry of hopeful anticipation — "O Great God, you alone truly know how it is possible for these dead words to become the Living Word!" After all, when God asks,

116

"Mortal, can these bones live?" this could be an expression of God's sense of humor — a playful poke in the ribs — in addition to God's bold challenge daring us to answer, "Yes, God can do indeed what to us mortals seems absolutely impossible!"

In order to understand how the example of the prophet Ezekiel could serve as a positive motivator whenever a biblical text seems dry and dull but yet impossible to simply discard, it is helpful to recall how events evolved in Ezekiel's vision of the valley of dry bones. Regardless of whatever anxiety, dread, or despair he may have felt regarding the sight of human bones strewn like roadside trash everywhere, Ezekiel did not protest or object when God quickly commanded him to prophesy boldly and cry out, "*O dry bones, hear the word of the Great and Living God*" (i.e., Ezekiel 37:4b in a manner once again using inclusive language). And we are told that in the prophet's vision these dead bones became connected and covered with flesh and skin, but — like the stiff and rigid figures in a wax museum — there was, as of yet, no life or breath in them. However, when Ezekiel obeyed God's urging him to "*prophesy to the breath*" (Ezekiel 37:9a), the skin and flesh-covered bones then were transformed into a huge host of living people. The whole house of Israel had been given a miraculous "jump start" and restored back to life again!

Let us now continue to imagine how our own experience with a seemingly dry and deadly biblical text could parallel Ezekiel's encounter with God in the valley of dry bones. When we can respond with a slow, grudging smile and somehow say,"Y-e-s," to God's fun-poking, bold challenge, "Can these bones live?" our "God only knows!" response can become a wholesome mix and healthy release of honest frustration, ironic humor, and revived anticipation. Once the death-like gridlock of our stifled imagination has been broken and shattered by our profuse, cathartic outpouring of frustration, humor, and hopeful anticipation, then through the grace of God we indeed may be blessed unexpectedly by a vision of some images and language tools which may have amazing potential to serve as "vital connections" between the scattered, seemingly useless bones of those "dry and deadly" biblical words. God's playful yet earnest challenge can jar us loose so that we now can begin

117

boldly to envision how this "most dull and deadly text" might actually become "*a live body*" — capable of generating excitement and enthusiasm within even the most slumber-addicted congregation! Just as Ezekiel was told to proclaim, "Oh dry bones, hear the word of the Great and Living God!" so we may be told to proclaim boldly (to ourselves at least!), "Let the dry bones of this impossible text contain *somehow* God's word that brings light and life to God's people!"

However, as we begin to write down our newly inspired ideas and insights, there, nevertheless, may still seem to be — h'mmm! something missing! — as our newly conceived imagery, plus all our available language tools, *somehow continue to fall short*. Perhaps we can begin to see how this difficult text has some possible connections now, but we aren't yet convinced that it is truly ready to take into the pulpit or the classroom. Somehow we may sense that we still are failing to make our most carefully connected images and words come truly alive and start to dance and vibrate with dynamic meaning and relevance. And so in the next phase of our coping with a difficult biblical text, we, like Ezekiel, may be instructed by God to "*prophesy to the breath*" by openly confessing and acknowledging that only the Spirit of God has what it definitely takes to breathe new life into this most extremely frustrating situation where we are desperately hanging "at the end of our rope." We may be amazed and astonished that miracles can actually happen whenever we become truly open and willing to let God use us as the chosen humble channels by which the Holy Spirit can breathe new life into even a most stubbornly difficult biblical text and thereby create vital, lively connections to our church members' most intense spiritual hurts and hunger.

So ... if we would seriously dedicate ourselves to carrying out a *prophetic* ministry, there is much we should learn from the prophet Ezekiel whose richly vivid imagination served as a fruitful channel for spiritual revelation. We often must obey God's command to address the "scattered bones" of extremely difficult biblical themes which, at first glance, may seem to have absolutely no living connections to our church members' spiritual needs, plus no inner "vital breath" that can inspire and generate an enthusiastic faith and commitment in the life of a congregation. When through the grace of God we have come up with language tools that can serve somehow as "wheels within the wheel" or "living connections" transforming dead bones into a flesh-and-blood body, we then are asked by God to "prophesy to the breath" by praying earnestly, *"Come, Holy Spirit, come!"* We are called to acknowledge freely and openly to ourselves and others that our Great God can be trusted to breathe new life and vitality into even those most difficult and demanding tasks of writing and *re-writing* which are absolutely indispensable for creating and refining the language tools urgently needed for faithful preaching and dedicated teaching.

Endnotes

1. Daniel Iverson, "Spirit of the Living God" (Birdwing Music — A Division of the Sparrow Corporation — copyright 1935, renewed 1963).

2. Paul Simon, "Bridge Over Troubled Waters," 1969.

3. Cecil Frances Alexander, "All Things Bright and Beautiful," 1848, Martin Shaw, arranger, 17th century English melody, 1915.

4. Cf., Sallie McFague, *Models of God: Theology for An Ecological, Nuclear Age* (Philadelphia: Fortress Press, 1987), pp. 78-87.

5. Geoff Love, "He's Got the Whole World in His Hands" (adaptation of a gospel song), 1958.

6. George Matheson and Albert L. Peace, "O Love That Will Not Let Me Go."

7. Cf., Leslie D. Weatherhead, *The Will of God* (New York: Abingdon Press: 1944), p. 20.

8. Leo Durocher, quoted in John Bartlett, *Bartlett's Familiar Quotations*, 16th Edition (Boston: Little, Brown and Company, 1992), p. 75.

9. Cf., Gian Carlo Menotti, *Amahl and the Night Visitors* (New York: William Morrow and Company Inc., 1986), pp. 56-59.

10. Cf., Elizabeth Johnson, *She Who Is: The Mystery of God in Feminist Theological Discourse* (New York: Crossroad, 1997), p. 100.

11. Edgar Bergen, *The Chase and Sanborn Hour*, radio show, NBC, 1937 (1939 — when Mortimer Snerd appeared).

12. Karl Barth, *Church Dogmatics: The Doctrine of the Word of God* (Edinburgh: T & T Clark, 1936), p. 339.

13. Cf., Johnson, *op.cit.*, p. 100.

14. *St. Paul's Cathedral: A Guide Prepared by the Cathedral* (section pertaining to the South Aisle), p. 18 (unnumbered).

15. Elton Trueblood, *The Humor of Christ* (New York: Harper & Row, Publishers, 1964), pp. 98-110.

16. *Ibid.*, pp. 15-32.

17. *Ibid.*, pp. 33-52.

18. *Ibid.*, pp. 68-69.

19. Henry F. Lyte and William H. Monk, "Abide With Me! Fast Falls the Eventide."

20. George Bennard, "The Old Rugged Cross."

21. Lewis E. Jones, "There Is Power in the Blood."

22. Charles Gabriel, "The Way of the Cross Leads Home."

23. George Whiting and Walter Donaldson, "My Blue Heaven," 1924.

24. Jerry Leiber and Mile Stoller, "Is That All There Is?" 1969.

25. Merle Travis, "Sixteen Tons," 1947.

26. Adapted from bumper sticker on sale in German Village bookstore, Columbus, Ohio.

27. Cf., Justin M. Glenn, "Sisyphus," *World Book Enclopedia*, 1994, XVII, 477. "Sisyphus was forced to roll a huge stone to the top of a hill. Each time Sisyphus was about to roll the stone over the summit, it pushed him back to the bottom of the hill."

28. Source unknown.

29. Kenneth Lee Asher and Paul Williams, "You and Me Against the World," Almo Music, 1974.

30. Howard Thurman, *Meditations of the Heart* (New York: Harper & Brothers, Publishers, 1953), p. 17.

31. James Rado, Gerome Ragni, and Galt MacDermot, "Let The Sunshine In" (from the musical *Hair* by James Rado, Lynn Kellogg, Meba Moore, and the Company), 1968.

32. Nancy Wood, *Many Winters* (Garden City, New York: Doubleday & Company, Inc., 1974), p. 46.

33. Thurman, *op. cit.*, p. 86.

34. W. D. Longstaff and George C. Stebbins, "Take Time to Be Holy."

35. Jay Livingston and Ray Evans, "To Each His Own," 1946.

36. Thomas Gordon, *P.E.T. Parent Effectiveness Training* (New York: David McKay, Inc., 1970), pp. 29-94.

37. John Fearis, "Beautiful Isle of Somewhere" (Dayton, Ohio: Lorenz Publishing Company, 1983).

38. Cf., James W. Fowler, *Stages of Faith* (San Francisco: Harper & Row, 1981), pp. 119-121.

39. Stephen Collins Foster, "Beautiful Dreamer," 1864.

40. Joe Darion and Mitch Leigh, "The Impossible Dream," 1965.

41. Cf., Fowler, *op. cit.*, pp. 122-134.

42. Cf., *ibid.*, pp. 135-150.

43. Katherine Hankey and William G. Fischer, "I Love to Tell the Story."

44. Cf., Fowler, *op. cit.*, pp. 151-173.

45. Cf., Erik H. Erikson, *Childhood and Society* (New York: W. W. Norton & Company, 1963), pp. 263-266.

46. Cf., Fowler, *op. cit.*, pp. 174-183.

47. Cf., Erikson, *op. cit.*, pp. 266-268.

48. Cf., Fowler, *op. cit.*, pp. 184-198.

49. Cf., Erikson, *op. cit.*, pp. 268-269.

50. Cf., Fowler, *op. cit.*, pp. 199-211.

51. Bruce Gilbert, producer, *On Golden Pond*, motion picture ITC/IPC, 1981.

52. "Old Time Religion," Author unknown, traditional (Grand Rapids, Michigan: Zondervan Publishing House).

53. Erikson, *op. cit.*, pp. 247-263.

54. Fowler, *op. cit.*, pp. 119-173.

55. W. S. Pitts, "The Little Brown Church In The Vale."

56. Irving Berlin, "White Christmas," 1942.

57. Words from country music song, title unknown.

58. "Now I Lay Me Down to Sleep," *The New England Primer*, 1784 quoted in John Bartlett, *Bartlett's Familiar Quotations*, 16th edition (Boston: Little, Brown and Company, 1992), p. 287: #14.

59. Jerry Siegel and Joe Shuster, *Superman*, TM & ©DC Comics.

60. John H. Sammis and Daniel B. Towner, "When We Walk with the Lord (Trust and Obey)."

61. "Death as a Comma" from unknown source submitted by Lou Bliss, Rochester, Vermont.

62. Katherine Hankey and William G. Fischer, *op. cit.*

63. Cf., James L. Christensen, *The Minister's Service Handbook* (Westwood, New Jersey: Fleming H. Revell Company, 1960), p. 31, and *Book of Worship: United Church of Christ* (New York: United Church of Christ Office for Church Life and Leadership, 1986), p. 80.

64. Cf., G. Cyprian Alston,"Low Sunday," *The Catholic Encyclopedia*, 1910, IX, 400-401.

65. Benjamin Franklin, quoted in John Bartlett, *Bartlett's Familiar Quotations*, 16th Edition (Boston: Little, Brown and Company, 1992), p. 310: #18.

66. Larry Morey and Frank Churchill, "Whistle While You Work" from Walt Disney, *Snow White and the Seven Dwarfs*, motion picture, 1937.

67. Thomas Gordon, *op. cit.*, pp. 194-215.

68. Hoagy Carmichael and Sidney Arodin, "Lazy River," 1931.

69. *The Love Boat*, television show, ABC, 1977.

70. "Old MacDonald," traditional folk song.

71. "Reach Out and Touch Someone," AT&T (long distance calling), listed in Laurence Urdang and Ceila Dame Robbins, editors, *Slogans* First Edition (Detroit: Gale Research Company, 1984), p. 332: #14.

72. Source unknown.

73. Paul Simon, "The Sounds of Silence," 1965.

74. Douglas McGregor, *The Human Side of Enterprise* (New York: McGraw Hill Book Company, 1960) cited in James H. Donnelly, Jr., James L. Gibson, and John M. Ivancevich, *Fundamentals of Management*, Third Edition (Dallas: Business Publications, Inc., 1978), pp. 178-179, p. 458.

75. "Trivial Pursuit," a Horn Abbot game licensed by Horn Abbot Ltd., owner of the registered trademark TRIVIAL PURSUIT, manufactured and distributed in the United States under license to Selchow & Richter Company.

76. *All in the Family*, television show, CBS, 1971.

77. Salvador Minuchin, *Families and Family Therapy* (Cambridge: Harvard University Press, 1974), pp. 46-66.

78. Bil Keane, *Family Circus*, cartoon feature, copyright Bil Keane, Inc., distributed by Cowles Syndicate, Inc.

79. Thomas A. Harris, *I'm OK — You're OK: A Practical Guide to Transactional Analysis* (New York: Harper & Row, Publishers, 1969), pp. 16-36.

80. Berlin, *op.cit.*

81. Richard B. Smith and Felix Bernard, "Winter Wonderland," 1934.

82. Gerhard Eberling, *Introduction to a Theological Theory of Language*, translated by R. A. Wilson (London: William Collins & Co. Ltd, 1973), p. 15.

83. Nancy Hardesty, *Inclusive Language in the Church* (Atlanta: John Knox Press, 1987), p. 16.

84. Samuel Laeuchli, *The Language of Faith: An Introduction to the Semantic Dilemma of the Early Church* (New York: Abingdon Press, 1962), p. 13.

85. Cf., *ibid.*, pp. 238-240.

86. Cf., Randolph Crump Miller, *The Language Gap and God: Religious Language and Christian Education* (Philadelphia: United Church Press, 1970), pp. 113-125.

87. Cf., *ibid.*, pp. 94-112.

88. Cf., *ibid.*, p. 130-133.

89. Carl Braater, editor, *Our Naming of God: Problems and Prospects of God-Talk Today* (Minneapolis: Fortress Press, 1989), p. 11.

90. Johnson, *op.cit.*, p. 7.

91. Sallie McFague, *Metaphorical Theology: Models of God in Religious Language* (Philadelphia: Fortress Press, 1982), p. 20.

92. Donald Moore, arranger, "Ezekiel Saw the Wheel," African-American Spiritual (Miami: Belwin-Mills Publishing Corporation, 1997).